SIMPLY SENSATIONAL
GLASS BEADING

DOROTHY WOOD

D&C
David and Charles

To Barley – I couldn't have done it without you.

A DAVID & CHARLES BOOK
David & Charles is a subsidiary of F+W (UK) Ltd.,
an F+W Publications Inc. company

First published in the UK in 2005

Distributed in North America
by F+W Publications, Inc.
4700 East Galbraith Road
Cincinnati, OH 45236
1-800-289-0963

A catalogue record for this book is available from the British Library.

ISBN 0 7153 1936 1 hardback
ISBN 0 7153 1937 X paperback

Printed in China by RRDonnelly
for David & Charles
Brunel House   Newton Abbot   Devon

Executive Editor Cheryl Brown
Editor Jennifer Proverbs
Art Editor Prudence Rogers
Production Controller Ros Napper
Project Editor Lin Clements
Photographer Simon Whitmore

Visit our website at www.davidandcharles.co.uk

David & Charles books are available from all good bookshops;
alternatively you can contact our Orderline on (0)1626 334555
or write to us at FREEPOST EX2 110, David & Charles Direct,
Newton Abbot, TQ12 4ZZ (no stamp required UK mainland).

Contents

Introduction

Beading is a traditional craft that has developed over the years to become one of the most popular hobbies, and this is in part due to manufacturers producing beads and sequins in fashionable colours and shapes. Beads can be simply added as an embellishment but if you really enjoy working with beads you can make beautiful completely beaded items, such as a sparkling crystal necklace or an amulet purse.

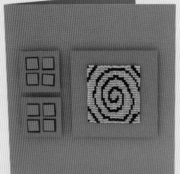

If you are new to beading, read through the first few pages of this book to learn a little about the innumerable sizes, colours and finishes of glass beads. This will give you confidence when you head off to the bead shop or craft store looking for beads for a particular project. Even if you don't have a bead shop in your area it is easy to buy beads by mail order as so many companies have their own website - look at the suppliers list on page 119 for details.

The bead projects in this book are divided into five chapters, each focusing on a different technique: bead loom work, bead embroidery, needle weaving, fringing, netting and tassels and, lastly, bead wirework. To illustrate the techniques there are some sensational card and gift tag designs which act as an introduction to each chapter and allow you to sample the technique. Beginners may like to start with one of these quick and easy designs or choose one of the simpler bead projects, such as the gift bags on page 40 or the night light holders on page 98. More experienced beaders can try their hand at the more advanced projects, such as the stunning cushion on page 26 or make a pair of beautiful dragonfly pins to match a favourite hat or outfit (page 108).

All the projects in the book have clear step-by-step instructions and list the colours and sizes of beads used so that you can substitute beads from your own supplies. If you are new to beading or just want to recreate one of the projects exactly, the precise bead details with code numbers are given on page 118.

Whatever your level of expertise, with over 35 projects, this book will keep you inspired and beading for a long time to come.

materials and equipment

It is very easy to get started working with glass beads because you don't need any specialist equipment initially - in fact all you need to begin is a needle and thread. Although it is possible to use any fine needle and thread, proper beading needles and thread will start you off in the right way as bead threads are much stronger and will prevent problems arising later. All the materials and equipment used in this book are readily available from craft or jewellery suppliers. If you don't have a local shop, check the supplier's list at the back of the book on page 119 to find companies who operate a mail-order system or have websites.

Needles

Beading needles have a flat eye that can pass through the small holes in seed beads. The two most common sizes are 10 and 13. Size 10 is a good standard needle, but if you are going to pass the needle through a bead several times, you will need the finer size 13. Short beading needles are ideal for embroidery but it is easier to use long beading needles for fringing, although they do bend and can break easily.

Thread

Polyester sewing thread is ideal for bead embroidery but a specialist beading thread is more suitable for other beading techniques. Nymo thread, available in a range of colours, is a strong, flat, nylon thread. The standard size D is suitable for most beadwork and the finer size B is ideal when passing the thread through a bead several times. Cord threads such as quilting thread are more suitable for making fringes and tassels as they allow the beads to swing attractively. Monofilament thread is a firm nylon thread that is ideal for bracelets and necklaces.

Thread conditioners

Thread conditioners strengthen and protect thread and make it less prone to tangling. It is not always necessary to condition threads when working with seed beads, but bugle and hex beads have sharp edges so condition your threads when using these. Run the thread through the conditioner, avoiding the needle area, and then pull the thread back through between your finger and thumb to remove any excess conditioner and smooth the thread.

Scissors

A sharp pair of embroidery scissors is useful for cutting thread to length and snipping off threads close to the beadwork. Use larger dressmaking scissors for cutting fabric.

Bead mats

Use a bead mat to spread beads out while you work, so you can discard any misshapen ones and pick the beads up easily on the needle. To make a mat, cut a piece of chamois leather or glue a square of velvet to card. The close pile on these materials prevents the beads from rolling away as you pick them up.

Jewellery findings

Choose the method of fastening your jewellery before you begin beading so that you leave enough thread to attach the findings or to make a bead fastening. Clasps and ear wires are readily available from bead suppliers. More unusual fastenings are available by mail order (see Suppliers).

Tassel tops

Bead tassel heads are worked over a wooden or plastic form to create the right shape. Tassel tops are available in a range of shapes and sizes from general craft suppliers. Use large round beads to make small beaded toggles and tassel heads.

Embroidery hoop

An embroidery hoop or frame keeps the fabric taut while you embroider with beads and prevents puckering.

Fabric markers

Use a water-soluble or vanishing-ink pen to mark out beading motifs on fabric before working bead embroidery.

Wire

Wire is used in beadwork when the beads have to hold a particular shape or if the wire is part of the decorative effect. Jewellery wire and coloured enamel wire are available in a wide colour range. Wire is either labelled with the standard wire gauge (swg) or measured in millimetres. Jewellery wire ranges from 0.2mm (36swg) to 1.2mm (18swg).

Pliers and wire cutters

If you plan to do lots of beading, it is worth investing in a set of jewellery tools as they are much finer than general tools and you will achieve better results. Bend wire with flat-nosed pliers or use them to pull the needle through a bead that is tightly packed with thread. Round-nosed pliers are used to bend wire to make loops and jump rings in a range of sizes. You can cut wire with most pliers but it is easier to cut close to the beadwork with wire cutters.

Bead looms

There are several different bead looms available; some are wooden and others have a wire frame. The wire spring or coil restricts the number of warp threads that can be strung on the loom and basic looms only have room for 30–35 beads. For weaving wider bands of beads you will need to buy or make a wider loom with a longer spring or coil.

Specialist tools

A spinster or cord maker (shown on page 22) is useful for twisting wire and making cords. It is a mini hand drill that speeds up the twisting process.

A jig is a plate with holes for pegs which allows you to bend wire into shape and repeat the shape again and again (see page 101). Jigs come in a range of shapes and can be made from metal or plastic. For a single project you could make one by simply hammering nails into a piece of wood.

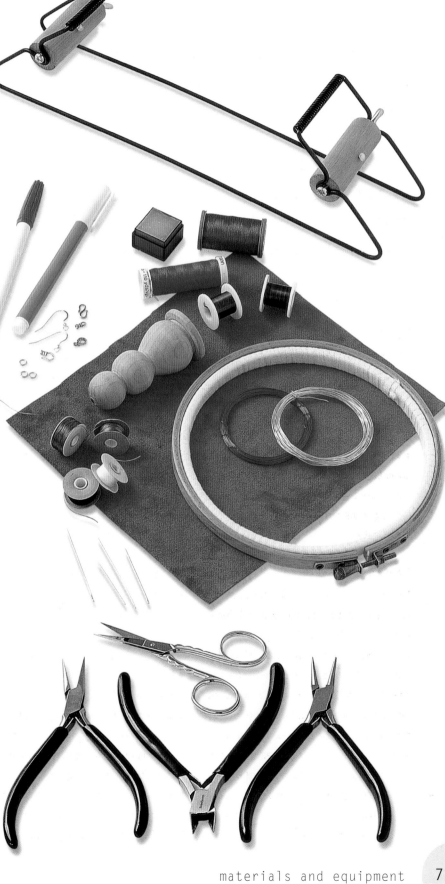

beads

At first sight all the beads in a bead shop look the same, but close inspection reveals a wide variety of shapes and sizes. When buying beads from a catalogue or on the web it helps to know the different types of beads and the names of the different finishes, as it is not always obvious what the beads actually look like from a photograph.

Seed beads are round, donut-shaped beads ranging in size from 5 to 15. Larger seed beads are known as **pony** beads and the smaller ones as **petites**. The most common sized seed beads are size 11 or 12.

Hex beads are cylindrical beads made from a six-sided glass cane. They are rather like a squat bugle bead and are very useful for creating texture.

Cylinder beads, also known by their trade names **Delicas**, **Antiques** and **Magnificas**, are precision-milled tubular beads. They are ideal for needle weaving and loom weaving as the beads sit next to one another and create an even bead fabric. They have a large hole enabling you to pass a needle and thread through each bead several times.

Bugle beads are made in a similar way to seed beads. The glass canes are cut to a variety of lengths from 2–30mm (1⁄16–1 1⁄4in). The most common sizes are 4mm (3⁄16in), 6mm (1⁄4in), 9mm (5⁄16in) and 15mm (5⁄8in). Twisted bugle beads are made from five- or six-sided tubes that have been twisted while the glass is still hot.

bead finishes

Beads often have two or more different descriptive words that explain exactly what the bead looks like. For example 'SL purple AB' is a silver-lined purple bead with an iridescent, rainbow effect on the surface (AB meaning aurora borealis). It's like a code system - once you know the code you can tell exactly what you are buying (see opposite, choosing and buying beads). The combinations of all of these different finishes produce a huge variety of different beads.

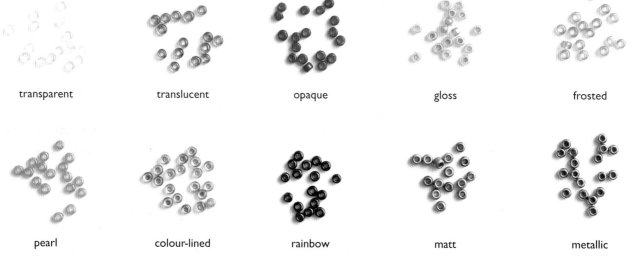

transparent   translucent   opaque   gloss   frosted

pearl   colour-lined   rainbow   matt   metallic

Transparent beads are made of clear or coloured glass which allows the light to pass through. Using a dark-coloured thread can therefore alter the colour of these beads.
Opaque beads are solid colour beads which don't allow any light to pass through.
Translucent beads are between transparent and opaque and are also known variously as greasy, opal and satin: **greasy** beads are made from cloudy glass; **opal** beads are slightly more transparent, while **satin** beads have tiny bubbles in the glass, which give the bead a directional sheen.

Gloss beads are very shiny, like glass.
Matt beads are opaque beads that have been tumbled or dipped in acid to produce a dull, flat surface.
Frosted beads are clear or translucent beads, which have been treated in a similar way.
Lustre beads have a transparent coating, either coloured or clear, giving them a subtle shine.
Ceylon beads have a milky, pearlized lustre.
Colour-lined (CL) beads have the hole in the bead lined with another colour. The beads can be clear or coloured.
Silver-lined (SL) beads have the hole in the

bead lined with silver and look very sparkly. These beads can be bleached to remove the silver lining leaving a more subtle finish.
Metallic beads include any bead that looks metallic. The finish can be painted on or, in the case of galvanized beads, the finish is electroplated to the bead surface. Beads with painted metallic finishes should not be washed. Iris or rainbow beads have been treated with metal salts to create a coating that resembles an oil slick. They are often made from dark or black opaque beads and are also known as aurora borealis (AB) beads.

choosing and buying beads

It has never been easier to buy beads because even if you don't have a bead shop nearby there are lots of mail order and internet companies to choose from. The beads are usually clearly illustrated, with precise details of their size, colour and finish. Look at the suppliers listed on page 119 for some useful addresses to get you started stocking up on your own supply of beads.

The quality of seed beads available varies, and you generally get what you pay for. The finest quality beads come from Japan, and this is often marked on the packet. When needle weaving or loom weaving it is essential to buy good quality beads that are of an even size, although it is fine to use less expensive beads for netting, fringing and coiling on wire.

Make use of your knowledge of the different types of beads when choosing them for your projects. Even if the beadwork appears to be all one colour, pick a selection of beads with different finishes to give the beadwork interest and vitality. You can use any size of seed bead for the projects although best results will be achieved using the correct size and type of bead specified in the text. For a unique finish, choose your own colours but if you would rather buy the exact beads used in the projects, full details are listed on page 118.

Seed beads, cylinder beads and bugles are sold in a variety of packets, bags and tubes with no standard bead packet sizes. The packets or containers usually have the weight of beads marked, making it easier to decide how many packets you require. Some beads are sold in round weights such as 5g or 100g; others are sold with a particular number of beads and so have an odd weight such as 4.54g. Unfortunately, the number of beads is not marked. Do check the weight of each different bead – some companies keep the bead quantity the same in each packet and vary the price, whereas others keep the price the same and alter the quantity.

Depending on the size or type of bead there are an average number of beads per gram so it is fairly easy to work out what quantity of beads you need for a certain project. Use the table below to help you work out how many beads you require.

Type of bead	Size of bead	5g bag (approx.)
Pebble bead	size 3	20
Pony bead	size 5	65
Seed bead	size 8	200
Seed bead	size 9	300
Seed bead	size 10	450
Seed bead	size 12	500
Petite bead	size 15	950
Cylinder bead	Delicas	800
Bugle bead	3mm	200
Bugle bead	7mm	150
Bugle bead	9mm	90
Bugle bead	15mm	55

pebble beads size 3   pony beads size 5   seed beads size 8

seed beads size 10   seed beads size 12

techniques

If you are new to beadwork it is worth working through this section to learn the skills required for some of the projects. Although most of the projects have full instructions enabling you to work the project from the step-by-step instructions, this section has useful tips and diagrams as well as detailed instructions for using a bead loom, embroidering with beads and all the needle weaving stitches used in the book.

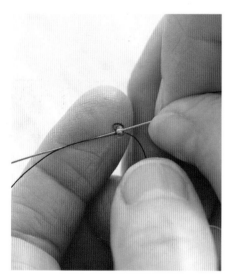

Beginning a piece of beadwork

Work with as long a length of thread as you can comfortably sew with to reduce the number of joins – between 1–2m (1–2yd) is ideal. Nymo thread is easier to thread straight off the reel. If you are using a round thread such as quilting thread, flatten the end and trim at an angle before threading the needle. To prevent thread from knotting, let the needle hang loose from time to time to unwind. If it does coil up and loop into a knot don't panic and pull the thread tight, simply put the needle into the loop and pull gently to one side to ease the knot out.

Using a 'stop bead' when needle weaving will stabilize the first row and prevent the beads from falling off. You can use the first bead in the row or use a bead in a different colour that can then be removed at a later stage.

To begin a piece of beadwork (left), pick up a bead and pass the needle back through it once or twice to anchor it. Leave a tail of at least 15cm (6in) for finishing off or adding a fastening.

Joining on another thread

Don't work right to the end of a thread. Leave a tail of 15cm (6in) to make it easier to attach a new thread and weave the ends back into the work.

1 In closely packed beadwork, weave the new thread backwards and forwards across the beadwork several times, bringing the new thread out through the same bead as the old thread. At a later stage, weave the old thread through the new beadwork in the same way and trim off the ends.

2 When working nets, chains or fringes, feed the needle back through several beads, secure the thread with a double half hitch (see page 23) and then feed the needle through several more beads before snipping off the end.

To join on another thread, reverse the process by feeding the new thread through several beads, tying a double half hitch and then bringing the needle out where you want to continue. A tiny drop of fray check liquid or a spot of clear nail varnish will secure the knot permanently.

bead loom weaving

Bead loom weaving is a quick method of producing flat bands of beading. The width of the band is only restricted by the loom width. Bead weaving on a loom produces a similar result to the square stitch in needle weaving. The beads are arranged in straight rows and so the design can be worked out on a square grid in the same way as cross stitch embroidery. There are two sets of threads on a bead loom: the warp threads run lengthways through the beadwork and are fitted to the loom, while the weft threads are crossways threads, which carry the beads and are woven in with a beading needle.

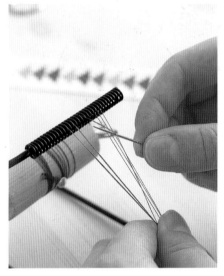

1 Count the number of beads across the design and add one to find the number of warp threads required. Add 60cm (24in) to the finished length of the project for attaching the threads to the loom and finishing off. Cut the warp threads and tie an overhand knot (see page 23) at one end.

2 Split the bundle in two and loop the knot over the little tack on the top roller. Loosen the wing nut and, holding the threads taut, wind the warp threads on to the roller, stopping when there is just enough thread to tie on to the other roller.

3 Hold the threads firmly and arrange along the top spring. Use a tapestry needle to sort one thread into each coil. Line the threads up across the bottom spring in the same way, so they run parallel to one another and don't cross at any point.

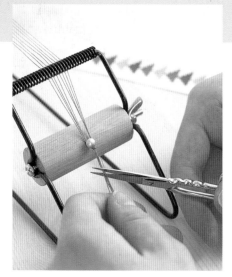

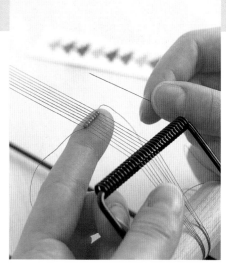

4 Tie an overhand knot and loop the knot over the tack on the bottom roller. Wind the rollers back until there is about 30cm (12in) on the bottom roller and then tighten the wing nuts at the sides.

5 Thread a needle with a 2m (2¼yd) length of thread and tie to the left-hand side warp thread with an overhand knot leaving a 15cm (6in) tail. Beginning at the bottom, read the beadwork chart from right to left and pick up the required number of beads in the right order.

6 Hold the beads under the warp threads and push them up between the warp threads so that there is a thread either side of each bead.

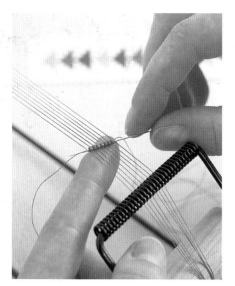

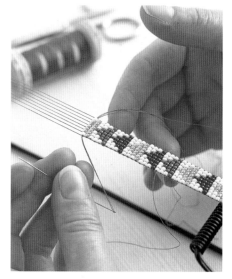

7 Feed the needle back through the beads from left to right, making sure that the needle passes on top of the warp threads. If the needle goes below the warp thread the beads will not be secured.

8 Pick up the next row of beads according to the chart and repeat the process, passing the needle back through the beads above the warp threads. After the first few rows it will become much easier to work.

9 When about 13cm (5in) of thread is left on the weft thread remove the needle and leave the thread hanging. Thread a new length and feed through five or six beads, leaving a 13cm (5in) tail. Weave ends in later.

A woven band brings a sumptuous look to this beautiful velvet pouch (see page 30).

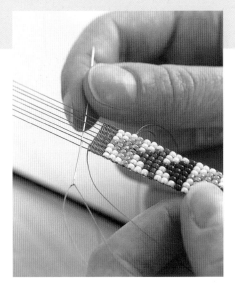 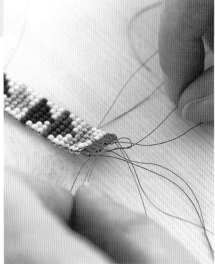 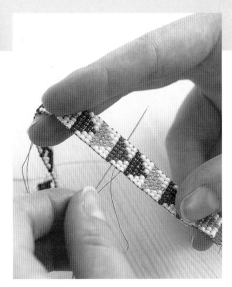

10 To finish the beadwork, weave the weft thread, without any beads on it, backwards and forward across the top of the beads to create a narrow fabric band. Roll the beadwork to the other end. Now attach another length of thread and weave this thread to create a narrow fabric band at the beginning of the beadwork.

11 Lift the beadwork off the loom. Tie pairs of warp threads together using a surgeon's knot (see page 23). Take the thread ends left over right, twice, and then right over left, twice, and pull tight. Trim the warp threads at each end to 6mm (¼ in)

12 Weave the ends of the thread into the beadwork for at least five beads and then double back for at least five beads. Trim the ends close to the beadwork on the reverse side.

needle weaving

Needle weaving is a way of stitching beads together to create a flat or tubular beaded fabric. There are lots of different stitches that can be used, each with distinct characteristics that determine the look and feel of the beadwork. The stitches may appear similar in samples but are not readily interchangeable as their different characteristics become evident in larger pieces. Brick stitch, ladder stitch, chain stitch, square stitch and peyote stitch are described below.

Brick stitch

Brick stitch is one of the easiest stitches to work and is so called because it looks like a brick wall. The stitch is flexible crossways but rather stiff lengthways and can be worked flat or in a tube. Begin with a foundation row of ladder stitch worked with a single needle as shown here or with two needles as shown opposite. You can use either seed beads or bugles.

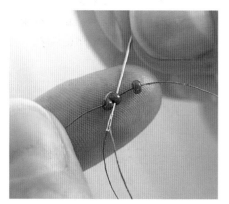

1 To make the foundation row pick up two seed beads and take the needle back through both beads. Open the beads out flat and pick up another seed bead. Take the needle through the previous bead and the one just added. Continue adding beads one at a time.

2 For the first row of brick stitch, pick up two beads and pass the needle under the first loop of thread between the first two beads on the foundation row. Pass the needle back through the second bead you picked up. Pick up another bead.

3 Pass the needle under the next loop and back through the bead again. Continue adding one bead at a time in this way to the end of the row.

4 Turn the beading round and pick up two beads to begin the next row. Repeat steps 2 and 3 until the beadwork is the size that you require.

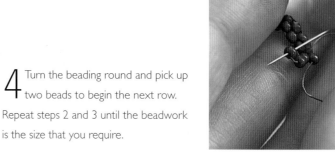

Ladder stitch

This simple stitch is often used to make the base for brick stitch. It is usually worked with bugle beads but seed beads can also be used. It can be worked with one needle (see brick stitch opposite) or with two needles as described here.

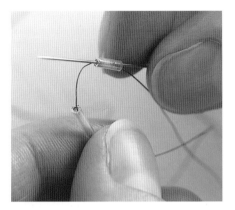

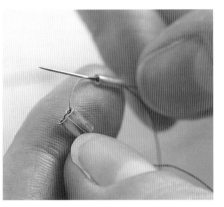

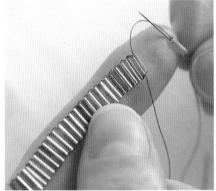

1 Cut a 2m (2¼yd) length of thread and thread a beading needle on to each end. Pick up two bugle beads on one needle and let them drop down to the middle of the thread. Now put the other needle through the second bead in the opposite direction.

2 Pull the threads tight. Pick up another bugle bead with one needle and put the other needle through the bead in the opposite direction.

3 Continue adding beads this way until the band is the length you require. To make the band into a tube, pass each needle through the first bead again and pull tight.

Chain stitch

Chain stitch (cable stitch) is ideal for making straps and can be embellished to make more ornate bracelets or necklaces. The number of beads can be varied in each chain to create different effects (see page 60).

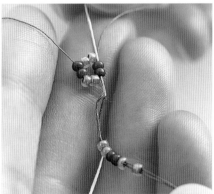

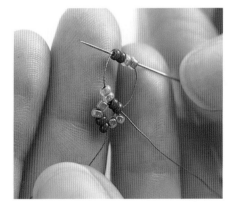

1 Pick up two light beads, two dark beads, two light beads and two dark beads. Tie the beads into a circle using a reef knot (see page 23), leaving a 15cm (6in) tail.

2 Pass the needle back through two dark, two light and two dark beads. Pick up two light, two dark and two light beads and put the needle back through the top two dark beads on the previous chain.

3 Pass the needle through the first two light and two dark beads just added, ready to add the next chain. Continue adding six beads at a time until the chain is the length you require.

Square stitch

Beads worked in square stitch look similar to beads woven on a loom. The needle passes through each bead several times and so you may need to use a size 13 needle and a fine thread in a toning colour. Square stitch is used to make the bead tubes for the retro torque on page 68.

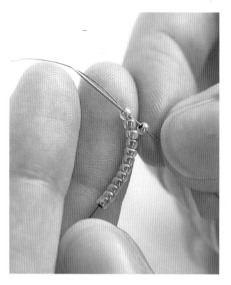

1 Pick up the required number of beads for the first row. For the second row, pick up a bead and pass the needle back through the last bead on the first row.

2 Pass the needle through the first bead on the second row again and back through the bead just added. The bead should be suspended below the first row.

3 Pick up a second bead and take the needle back through the second last bead on the previous row. Continue working along the row adding on one bead at a time.

4 To strengthen the fabric, at the end of the row go back through the previous row and the one just worked, ready to begin the next row.

Peyote stitch

Peyote stitch is a versatile stitch that is easiest to work with an even number of beads in each row. It is an ideal stitch for bags with a flap, such as the amulet purse on page 72, as the fabric is very flexible along its length.

Joining pieces of beadwork

Sometimes it is necessary to make a seam and join two pieces of beadwork and in beadwork it is possible to make an invisible join. Square stitch and peyote stitch have flat sides and can be butted together. Pass the needle and thread through one bead at a time alternating from side to side to join the seam.

To join pieces of brick stitch or when making a tube with peyote stitch, it is necessary to slot the two pieces together using the beads jutting out in the alternate rows, as shown below. Put the needle through the jutting-out bead on one side. Take it through the jutting-out bead on the opposite side and pull tight. Continue working down the seam in this way.

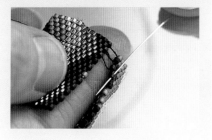

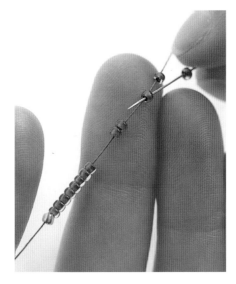

1 Pick up a bead and anchor it with a stop bead (see page 12) leaving a 15cm (6in) tail. Pick up an even number of beads to give the required width for the first row. Pick up a bead, and missing the last bead on the first row, pass the needle through the next bead.

2 Pick up another bead, miss a bead on the first row and pass the needle through the next bead. Continue to the end of the row missing every second bead. Pull the thread tight so beads sit alternately in pairs and single beads along the length in a zigzag pattern.

3 Work backwards and forwards in the same way, picking up one bead at a time and passing the needle through the next 'dropped-down' bead until the beading is the required length.

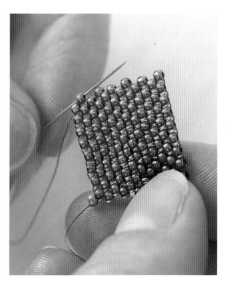

4 To decrease, don't pick up a bead at the beginning of the row but take the needle through the last dropped-down bead of the previous row, and then continue on as before.

bead embroidery

Bead embroidery transforms everyday objects into luxury items. There are several stitches that can be used to attach beads in different ways. Beads can be attached individually, in groups or in rows to most fabrics. The important thing about bead embroidery is that the thread needs to be strong and must be secured carefully so the beads don't fall off in use.

Preparing to embroider

• You can embroider on almost any fabric, from the finest silks to heavy felts and blanket fabrics.

• Thicker fabrics can be stitched without stretching but if the fabric is flimsy it needs to be supported in an embroidery hoop or frame while working so the beadwork doesn't scrunch up.

• Backing fabrics are useful for supporting bead embroidery and can be used to anchor threads on the reverse side. Backing fabrics should be chosen to suit the weight and handle of the top fabric.

• If the beaded fabric is being used to cover a box, for example, you can also use an iron-on interfacing instead of backing fabric and embroider even lightweight fabrics without a hoop.

• Begin beadwork with backstitches rather than a knot and use a strong thread that won't break easily.

Attaching beads

Beads can be stitched individually, in small groups or in long rows. The method used to attach beads depends on their size, the design of the beadwork and personal preference. Use a single strand of a strong thread such as Nymo or quilting thread, or two strands of ordinary sewing thread.

 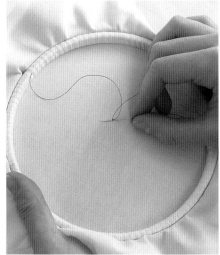

1 Cut the fabric and any backing fabric at least 5cm (2in) larger all round than the finished piece. Fit the fabric into an embroidery hoop or on to a rotary frame.

2 Take two tiny backstitches on the reverse side and bring the needle out on the right side where you want the beadwork to begin. You are now ready to start your bead embroidery.

Straight stitch

Individual beads can be added in embroidery with a simple straight stitch. This stitch is ideal for filling in areas with randomly placed beads, whether they are closely packed or scattered over the surface. In general you should choose your thread to match the beads rather than the background fabric. If, however, the beads are to be widely spaced then the thread may be visible through the fabric and in this case use a thread to match the fabric.

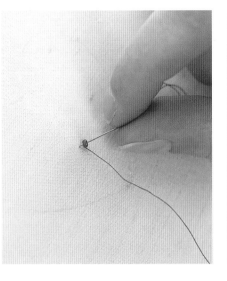 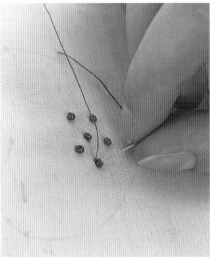

1 Secure the thread on the reverse side and bring the needle out where the bead is to be attached. Pick up a single bead and take the needle back through a bead length away from where it first emerged.

2 When adding individual beads that are spaced out it is better to work two straight stitches through each bead to prevent beads being pulled out.

Backstitch

Backstitch is generally used as an alternative to couching, although it is useful for attaching two or three beads in a row. When working long lines of beads, only pick up one or two beads at a time to follow a curved line but on a straighter line pick up five or six, taking the needle back through the last one or two beads each time.

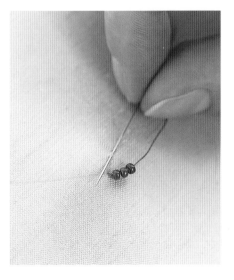 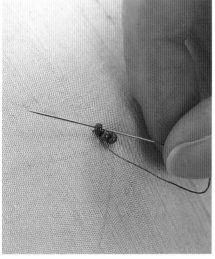

1 Pick up several beads and drop them down to where the thread emerges. Put the needle back into the fabric at the end of the row. Take a small backstitch and bring the needle out between the last two beads.

2 Put the needle back through the last bead and then pick up several more beads ready to begin again.

Couching

Couching is used to apply a string of beads to fabric in a straight line or a curve. You need to use two needles on separate lengths of thread – one beading needle and one sewing needle. You can stitch between each individual bead or every two to three depending on the tightness of the curved line.

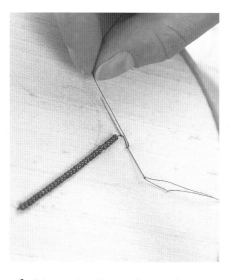

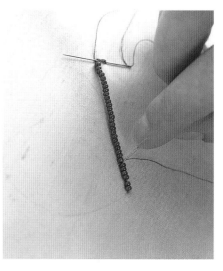

1 Bring the beading needle out where you want the beadwork to begin. Pick up sufficient beads to complete the line. If the beads are being couched in a straight line, put the beading needle in the fabric and wrap the thread around to hold the beads taut.

2 Bring the second thread out between the first and second beads. Take the thread over the bead string and back through the fabric. Work down the bead strand, stitching between the beads. At the end take both threads to the reverse side and secure them.

Making a cord

When you make small gift bags such as those on page 40, it can be quite a challenge to find a cord that is a suitable weight or colour for the design. It is often much easier to use embroidery cotton (floss) or metallic threads to make your own. Use a pencil or a spinster cord-making tool to twist the threads together.

1 Remembering that the threads will be doubled up, cut sufficient lengths of embroidery cotton (floss) two and a half times the length of the finished cord. Fold the threads in half and tie a knot. Secure the knot end to a door handle or similar.

2 Fit a spinster hook or pencil in the loop at the other end and twist the cord until it begins to coil up on itself. Holding the cord taut, fold it in half and let it twist up. Tie the ends together then run the cord between finger and thumb to even out any kinks.

knots used in beading

There are several simple knots used in beading to anchor threads or for tying off ends securely and it is worthwhile learning these knots so that your beadwork remains intact and fastenings firmly attached during use. For extra security use a cocktail stick to drop a tiny amount of fixative on the knots, such as clear nail polish or a fray check liquid.

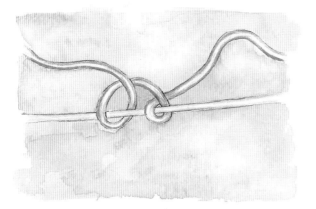

Double half hitch

Use this knot to secure a thread in netting or fringes before feeding the end through several more beads and trimming the end.

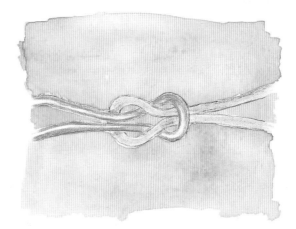

Reef (square) knot

This is the basic knot for joining two threads of equal thickness. Feed each end back through several beads before trimming the ends.

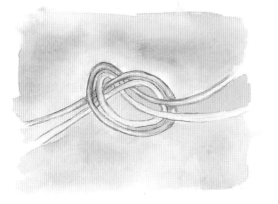

Overhand knot

Use this knot to tie threads together before fitting on a bead loom or to join two threads together at the edge of a piece of work. The knot can be easily manoeuvred into position with a needle.

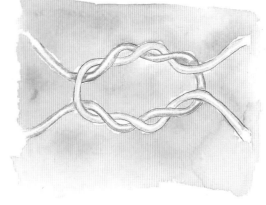

Surgeon's knot

This knot is similar to a reef knot but each thread end is taken over and under twice. The knot is more secure than a reef knot and doesn't loosen while it is being tied.

Bead loom weaving

Bead loom weaving is a simple technique that can create an infinite number of different bead patterns. Designs can be bold and abstract, such as the stunning bead panel made for the gorgeous cushion on page 26 or have an understated motif as used to decorate the beautiful velvet pouch on page 30. Seed beads vary in size as well as quality and it is essential to buy top quality, even-sized beads for bead loom weaving. The best beads are the cylinder beads, also known as delicas, antiques or magnificas, although you can pick out uneven

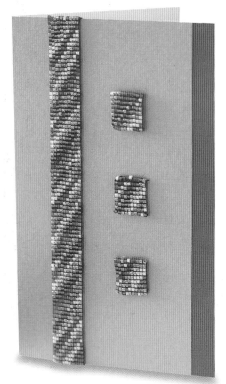

Abstract stripes

Work a narrow panel and three small squares from the cushion chart on page 112 to create this stunning yet simple card.

You could add a greeting down the pink border using rub-down transfers or peel-offs.

You will need

- delica beads in lined crystal medium pink, lined crystal rose lustre, transparent tangerine AB, semi-matt silver-lined orange, matte transparent orange
- pink quilting thread
- bead loom
- 14.5 x 9cm (5¾ x 3½in) single-fold orange pearlescent card
- 14.5 x 9cm (5¾ x 3½in) piece of pink pearlescent card
- craft knife, ruler and cutting mat
- wide double-sided tape

Create this card by first setting up the bead loom with 11 threads (see page 13). Photocopy the chart from page 112 and mark a section 10 beads wide. Work the bead panel until it is 14.5cm (5¾in) long. Leave a 5cm (2in) gap and then work nine rows of the pattern. Repeat twice more to make three small squares in all. Cut the small square panels from the loom and carefully stick the threads on the reverse side with tape.

Trim 1cm (½in) from the front right-hand edge of the orange card. Lay the long bead panel about 1.5cm (⅝in) from the fold and use double-sided tape to stick the threads to the back. Stick the pink card on the reverse side of the orange card so a 1cm (½in) border juts out. Use tape to stick the beaded squares on the front of the card as shown.

beads from regular seed beads. As its name suggests, bead loom weaving is worked on a bead loom. There are several styles, available in a range of widths (see page 7). Clear step-by-step instructions on using a bead loom are outlined on page 13 and specific details given on the project pages. If you have never worked with a bead loom, you could try a smaller section from the project charts and then use the beadwork to make one of the stunning greeting cards shown here.

Any bead design can be worked out on a square grid, although some adjustment will need to be made for the size and shape of bead. To work out how much to adjust, simply weave a small square panel of the beads and count the rows across and down.

Mackintosh Rose

Take a small section of the Charles Rennie Mackintosh bead panel on page 34 to create a striking card which is perfect for any occasion.

You will need

- delica beads in lined fuchsia and black
- pink quilting thread
- bead loom
- 13cm (5¼in) square pink single-fold card
- small scraps of black, pink and orange card
- 3-d sticky fixers
- wide double-sided tape

Create this card by first setting up the bead loom with 31 threads (see page 13). Photocopy the chart from page 114 and draw a square 30 beads wide and 25 beads high. Although part of the chart will include purple beads, work the whole design in pink and black. Lift the bead panel off the loom and stick the threads to the reverse side using double-sided tape.

Cut a 6.5cm (2½in) square of orange card and stick the bead panel in the middle using double-sided tape. Cut two 3cm (1¼in) squares in orange and stick four small black squares, topped with slightly smaller pink squares on each to create a grid pattern, as shown. Mount all three panels on the card using 3-d sticky fixers.

It is easier to use a wide double-sided tape to stick the bead panels to the card.

Vibrant cushion

Cushions are one of the most useful items of soft furnishing and can be used in any room. Arranged on the sofa, tucked in the corner of a favourite chair or strewn on a bed, they add a wonderful touch of colour. Work this gorgeous abstract bead panel in a stunning colour to suit your décor and choose a luxurious fabric such as a vibrant silk dupion to show off the tiny delica beads. As the design is abstract it is easy to adapt - you could make a narrower bead panel or just work a small section on the bead loom to create a small gift or card, as described on page 24. See page 29 for two more vibrant cushion colours.

You will need

(bead details page 118)

- 5g each of delica beads – lined sky blue AB, lined light blue AB, lined crystal light aquamarine, dyed matt transparent aquamarine and matt opaque royal blue
- blue Nymo thread
- size 10 long beading needle
- bead loom
- masking tape
- 0.5m (½yd) bright blue silk dupion
- 28cm (11in) length of 4cm (1½in) wide blue linear ribbon
- fusible bonding web
- matching sewing thread
- sewing machine
- 30 x 45cm (12 x 18in) cushion pad

quick idea ***Abstract Card*** *Work just a small section of the bead panel to create this contemporary card, described fully on page 24.*

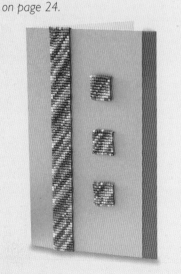

1 Set up the bead loom with thirty-one 86cm (34in) lengths of blue Nymo thread (see bead loom weaving page 13). Following the blue beadwork chart on page 112, work a length of beadwork to fit across your cushion. My band is approximately 25cm (10in) long and just over four repeats of the pattern. If you are working one of the other colourways, follow the appropriate chart on page 113.

2 Weave a thread panel at both ends of the completed bead panel before lifting it off the loom. Sew in any side threads. Secure the bead panel to the work surface with masking tape and tie the thread ends together in pairs using a surgeon's knot (see page 23).

3 Cut the blue linear ribbon down the middle and, if your ribbon is wire-edged, pull the wire out. Cut two strips of fusible bonding web and iron on to the back of the two ribbon strips.

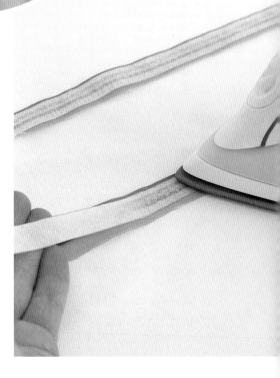

4 Cut a 28 × 46cm (11 × 18in) piece of blue silk and fold in half across the width to mark the centre line. Pin the ribbon pieces either side of the folded line so there is a 4cm (1½in) gap between the decorative blue lines on the ribbon.

If your silk is too lightweight to support the bead panel, back the fabric with a lightweight interfacing before you begin.

5 Pin the bead panel across the silk so it is positioned centrally between the ribbon strips. Using matching sewing thread, stitch the panel on to the cushion cover top using small stitches every two or three beads.

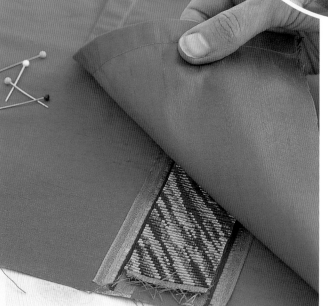

6 To make the cushion back, cut two 25 × 28cm (10 × 11in) pieces of blue silk. Turn over a 1.25cm (½in) double hem along a long edge of each piece and press. Machine stitch the hem. Lay the cushion top right side up. Pin one of the silk panels to one end with right sides together and the other panel to the other end, so that they overlap.

7 Fit a zipper foot on the machine and machine stitch around the edge of the cover so the stitching is exactly along the edge of the bead panel. Trim across the corners and turn the cover through. Ease out the corners and press. Insert the cushion pad through the envelope opening.

try this *Luscious Colourways* To make stunning pink or lime cushions, follow the instructions for the blue cushion but use the alternate charts on page 113 and bead colours on page 118. Alternatively, create a vibrant colour scheme of your own.

Antique velvet pouch

This unusual pouch is a wonderful mix of old and new. It has a contemporary look but the choice of fabric and ribbon in this beautiful mellow yellow give it an almost antique feel which makes it ideal whether you have a modern pad or a luxurious boudoir. Look out for this unusual ruffled ribbon which is available from specialist ribbon shops (see Suppliers page 119); this frames the bead panel and softens the edges so that the whole design holds together. Choose a really beautiful button or some pretty ribbon trim to finish off the pouch, which can be used to keep make-up, jewellery or other paraphernalia in one place.

antique velvet pouch

You will need
(bead details page 118)

- 5g each size 11 seed beads – pale peach, frosted gold, frosted apricot, desert sand, gold, Victorian gold, bronze, pearl, peachy blush, cream and vanilla

- 8g each size 11 seed beads – crystal honey and frosted autumn

- white Nymo thread

- bead loom

- size 10 beading needle

- 46 × 28cm (18 × 11in) yellow velvet

- 46 × 28cm (18 × 11in) yellow silk dupion

- 50cm (20in) length of 1.25cm (½in) wide dark cream ruched ribbon

- matching sewing thread

- sewing machine

- masking tape

- 40cm (16in) each of narrow gold organza ribbon and gold silk ribbon

1 Cut twenty-two 90cm (35in) lengths of white Nymo thread. Tie an overhand knot (see page 23) in one end and fit into the bead loom (see page 13). Work the bead design following the chart on page 114. Weave thread backwards and forwards across each end of the bead panel to make a 6mm (¼in) band. Lift the panel off the loom and sew in the side threads. Secure the panel to the work surface with masking tape and tie the ends together in pairs using a surgeon's knot (see page 23).

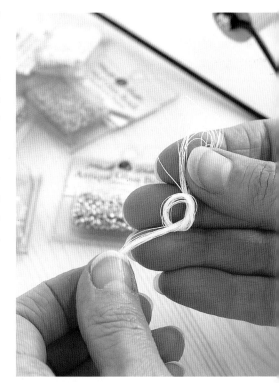

2 Cut two 23 × 28cm (9 × 11in) pieces of yellow velvet and two pieces of silk dupion the same size. Pin two 25cm (10in) lengths of ruched ribbon across one of the velvet pieces about 4cm (1½in) from the bottom edge and with a 3.2cm (1½in) gap between them for the bead panel.

If you can't find ruched ribbon, pre-gathered narrow lace would also look great.

3 Tack (baste) along the ribbon border to secure it to the velvet. Pin the bead panel between the ruched ribbons and use matching sewing thread to stitch in place with tiny stitches every two or three beads.

4 Pin a piece of silk dupion to the top edge of a piece of velvet with right sides facing and machine stitch. Do the same with the other pieces of silk and velvet. Press the seams open. With right sides facing, pin and tack (baste) the two pieces together, matching the seam lines. Fit a zipper foot into the machine so you can stitch as close as possible to the bead panel. Stitch around the edge, leaving a large gap for turning on one side of the lining.

5 Trim the seams and across the corners, then turn through. Roll the top edge between your fingers and thumbs so the seam is exactly on the edge and press with a steam iron. Fold over the top edge and mark the position of the ribbon fastening.

To make seams less bulky when the pouch is turned through, trim the seam allowances on the velvet to 6mm (¼in).

6 Cut the narrow organza and silk ribbons in half. Thread a piece of each into a large needle and tie a knot in the end. Feed the needle through the gap in the lining and out at the centre of the top edge. Bring the second lengths of ribbon out on the pouch at the mark. Slipstitch the gap and tie the ribbons in a bow to fasten.

Mackintosh rose album

Charles Rennie Mackintosh designs are as fresh today as when they were created over 100 years ago and the simple style, often used for stained-glass windows, is ideal for bead loom work. This elegant beaded panel, worked in Mackintosh's favourite pink, purple and green, could also be used to decorate a notebook or evening bag. Choose tones of silk dupion that show off the beaded panel and bind the album pages with bright green cord. The binding is tied in a Japanese style, which reflects how Mackintosh was influenced by Oriental art and design. Try applying just the rose motif to a quick card project, described fully on page 25.

You will need

(bead details page 118)

- 5g each of delicas –
  black, lined magenta AB, lined
  crystal fuchsia and green iris
- purple quilting thread
- bead loom
- size 10 beading needle
- masking tape
- gummed tape
- wide double-sided
  adhesive tape
- 23 x 14cm (9 x 5½in) photo
  album kit (see Suppliers)
- two 22.5 x 13.5cm
  (8¾ x 5¼in) pieces of
  cartridge paper
- 20 x 40cm (8 x 16in)
  pink silk dupion
- 20cm (8in) square wine
  silk dupion
- 23 x 28cm (9 x 11in)
  lo-loft wadding (batting)
- 1m (1yd) green cord
- bodkin

quick idea — **Rose Card** *If you are short of time why not create this pretty card using just the rose motif, described fully on page 25.*

1 Set up the bead loom with thirty-four 76cm (30in) lengths of purple quilting thread (see bead loom weaving, page 13). Following the beadwork chart on page 114, work the bead design. Weave a 6mm (¼in) band of thread across each end of the bead panel and then lift it off the loom. Sew in any side threads.

2 Secure the panel to the work surface with masking tape and tie the ends of the threads together in pairs using a surgeon's knot (see page 23). Stick a piece of double-sided tape along the top and bottom edges of the panel on the back. Fold the thread band back on to the tape and then trim the threads.

Instead of using a photo album kit, look out for a suitable ready-made album and re-cover it in silk as described in the stepped instructions.

3 To make the album cover, select the thick card pieces from the album kit and join the small and large pieces of card together with brown gummed tape so there is a 6mm (¼in) gap. Stick a second piece of tape on the reverse side.

4 Cut a piece of lo-loft wadding (batting) the same size as the cover and stick in place on the right side of the album with double-sided tape. Cut two 18 x 20cm (7 x 8in) pieces of pink silk and use these to cover the front and back album covers, sticking in place with double-sided tape and mitring the corners neatly. Cut two 10 x 18cm (4 x 7in) pieces of wine silk. Fold under 1cm (½in) along one long edge of each and stick across the album to cover the raw edge of the pink fabric.

5 Mitre the corners of the wine silk neatly, stick double-sided tape around the inside edge and stick the silk to the inside. Cut two 22.5 x 13.5cm (8¾ x 5¼in) pieces of cartridge paper and stick on the inside of the covers to hide the raw edges.

6 Use wide double-sided tape or spray adhesive to stick the beaded panel to the front of your album.

7 Use a large needle or fine embroidery scissors to punch holes through the silk and paper. Fold up the paper inserts and weigh down for an hour or so. Assemble the album and then, using a bodkin or large needle, bring the green cord up through one hole, leaving a 20cm (8in) tail at the back. Take the cord over the end of the album and then over the side edge. Take the cord diagonally over the end, to come up through the other hole. Repeat the process on this hole and then take the cord diagonally over the end of the album, tie the ends together neatly and snip off the excess cord.

mackintosh rose album

Bead embroidery

Embroidery is the most tactile way to add beads as an embellishment and the designs can be as simple or complicated as you like. One of the easiest ways to begin bead embroidery is to work a simple design along a piece of ribbon, a technique used for the fabulous gift bags on page 40.

This simple technique has also been used to great effect to make the gorgeous special occasion card and gift tag below. Making cards is a great way to use up beads left over from other projects, such as the lace pillow and sachet on pages 44 and 49. These show how easy it is to adapt

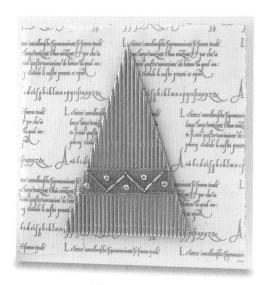

Golden triangles

Using embroidered ribbon is a very quick and easy way to add beads to a greetings card or gift tag.

You will need

- 1.5cm (⅝in) gold mesh ribbon
- gold corrugated card triangle 10.5 x 7cm (4⅛ x 2¾in)
- petite gold seed beads
- 7mm gold bugles
- 4mm gold beads
- pins
- size 10 beading needle
- gold sewing thread
- gold script vellum
- deckle-edged scissors
- 14cm (5½in) square ivory pearlescent card
- 3-d sticky fixers
- double-sided tape

Create this card by first wrapping a piece of gold ribbon around the gold triangle about 2cm (¾in) from the base and fixing on the back with double-sided tape. Using pins, mark the centre of the ribbon along the top edge and divide the lower edge into three. Bring a threaded needle out at one edge of the ribbon, pick up a petite seed bead and a bugle, repeat and then pick up a third petite bead. Take a tiny stitch at the first pin on the lower edge and bring the thread back up through the last petite bead. Work along the ribbon adding the same bead sequence to create a zigzag. Bring the needle out in the middle of one of the small triangles, pick up a 4mm gold bead and a petite seed bead, and take the needle back through the gold bead. Work along the ribbon adding the same beads in each triangle.

Using deckle-edged scissors, cut gold script vellum to fit the card front and stick in place with double-sided tape. Attach the bead panel with 3-d fixers.

Make a matching gift tag with a gold corrugated card triangle, punching a hole at the top for ribbon.

designs. The pillow will take a few days to make, but you can make the sachet in a matter of hours or simply create a beautiful heart card for a wedding or Valentine's Day (see below).

Bead embroidery always looks best if the beads tone with or match the background fabric, as the contrast of textures will always ensure the beads stand out. The picture frame and padded box on pages 50 and 55 use toning beads to create designs that have a professional finish and although handmade do not have the 'home-made' look. For best results, read the techniques on page 20 first.

Glittering heart

Aperture cards are the traditional way to mount a piece of bead embroidery. Look out for unusual-shaped apertures or cut your own from pretty card.

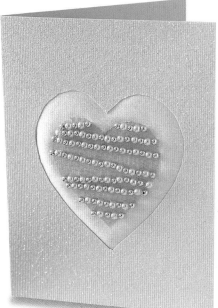

You will need

- 2mm gold beads
- 4mm ivory pearls
- small piece of ivory silk dupion
- small piece of backing fabric
- small piece of gold metallic organza
- small piece of thin wadding (batting)
- embroidery hoop
- fusible bonding web
- size 10 beading needle
- sewing thread
- 27 x 11.5cm (10¾ x 4½in) gold glitter card

Create this card by first tracing a heart shape from the template on page 115 on to fusible bonding web. Iron on to the metallic organza and cut out. Peel off the backing paper and iron the heart on to the ivory silk dupion and then tack (baste) the dupion on to the backing fabric. Bring the needle out near the bottom of the heart and pick up sufficient alternate gold beads and pearls. Take the needle back through to the other side. Couch over the beads once to secure. Work up the heart adding lines of beads and pearls, couching them down every two or three beads.

Score the glitter card every 9cm (3½in) and fold along the lines. Enlarge the heart template slightly and use it to cut out a heart from the middle of the centre panel. Cut a heart shape the same size in wadding (batting). Stick double-sided tape around the inside of the aperture. Position the beading behind it and press. Lay the wadding behind the heart and stick the flap down.

Try to begin and finish each line with the same beads to make the overall design more pleasing to the eye.

Sumptuous gift bags

These bags are so gorgeous they are almost a gift in themselves - you will only need some tissue paper to wrap one or two bits and bobs to make a substantial present. Look for unusual lightweight fabrics for interesting texture, such as this crushed polyester, and find a pretty ribbon that can be beaded for the bottom. Rather than searching for matching cord and tassels, choose stranded embroidery cotton (floss) the same shade as the bag and make your own following the instructions on page 22. The bags are shown in blue and pink colourways: to make the blue version, simply reverse the colours when following the main instructions.

You will need

for the pink bag

(bead details page 118)

- 32 × 24cm (12½ × 9½in) pink crushed polyester fabric
- 1.5cm (⅝in) deep pink organza ribbon
- sewing thread to match fabric
- size 13 beading needle
- 1g pink-lined size 10 seed beads
- forty size 10 bright blue seed beads
- 1g pink-lined 7mm bugles
- six pink-lined 4mm square beads
- five bright blue 4mm square beads
- stranded cotton (floss) deep pink DMC 3804 or Anchor 63
- spinster tool or pencil

try this *Cool Blue Bag Create this alternative colourway to the hot pink. Use blue crushed polyester, deep blue organza ribbon and reverse the bead colours – page 118 gives the alternative bead codes.*

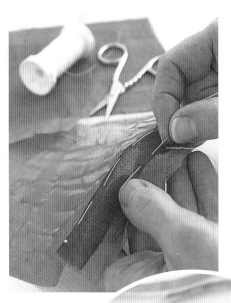

1 Cut two 32 × 12cm (12½ × 4¾in) pieces of polyester fabric. Tack (baste) a 12cm (4¾in) length of organza ribbon across one end, 1cm (⅜in) from the edge. With right sides together, machine stitch around all sides without catching the ribbon and leaving a gap on one side seam for turning the bag through.

2 Trim the seams to 3mm (⅛in) and trim across corners to reduce bulk. Turn the bag through to the right side and press the ribbon end to the halfway point. Slipstitch the gap. Tuck the 'lining' end inside and carefully press the top edge.

Check the fibre content of unusual fabrics such as the crushed sheers used on these bags, so you can use the correct iron temperature to press seams without damaging the fabric.

3 Thread a beading needle with a double length of sewing thread and tie a knot in one end. Bring the needle out in the middle of the ribbon at one side. Pick up a pink seed bead, a pink square bead and a pink seed bead. Backstitch through the last seed bead.

4 Pick up a pink bugle and a pink seed bead and backstitch to secure at 45 degrees to the other beads. Take a tiny stitch to bring the needle back out just below the seed bead and pick up another bugle and seed bead. Backstitch to form the second side of the diamond. Repeat to finish the diamond shape.

5 Bring the needle out at the inside edge of the diamond. Pick up a turquoise seed bead, a square turquoise bead and a turquoise seed bead and sew in place, bringing the needle out at the outside of the diamond. Pick up a pink square bead and a pink seed bead and backstitch. Repeat steps 4 and 5 to make five diamonds across the ribbon.

6 To make the cord, cut four 110cm (43in) lengths of stranded cotton (floss) and follow the instructions for making a cord on page 22.

7 Wrap stranded cotton (floss) around three fingers 14 times and cut at one side. Lay the strands flat and lay the cord down the centre with the knot in the middle. Tie a thread tightly round the strands and cord above the knot. Adjust the strands around the cord and let the top strands fall down. Wrap thread around below the knot to form the neck.

8 To finish, sew two rings of 10 blue seed beads around each tassel neck and secure the threads inside the head.

Luxurious lace pillow

Handmade cotton lace is an essential element in this beautiful beaded pillow as it has a wonderful softness and luxurious quality that frames the beadwork to perfection. You can gather a single layer of lace around the border but using a double layer in two different widths gives the pillow an almost decadent feel. The beadwork design uses two subtly different shades of pearls in ivory and cream which lift the design, while petite seed beads add a touch of sparkle. If you want to use the pillow as a bridal ring pillow, sew a length of ribbon to the centre of the pillow to tie the wedding rings to.

luxurious lace pillow

You will need
(bead details page 118)

- Two 30cm (12in) squares of ivory silk dupion
- 30cm (12in) square of white cotton backing fabric
- 150 (approx) 3mm ivory pearls
- 350 (approx) 1.5mm cream pearls
- 3g size 11 vanilla seed beads
- 2g petite crystal seed beads
- 25cm (10in) diameter embroidery hoop
- water-soluble marker
- size 10 beading needle and a sewing needle
- tacking (basting) thread and ivory sewing thread
- 30cm (12in) square of interfacing
- polyester stuffing
- pot-pourri sachet
- 2m (2¼yd) of 8cm (3in) wide cotton lace
- 2m (2¼yd) of 5cm (2in) wide cotton lace
- 2m (2¼yd) of 2cm (¾in) wide cotton lace
- 1m (1yd) of 6mm (¼in) wide cream satin ribbon
- 1m (1yd) of 6mm (¼in) wide cream organza ribbon
- glass-headed pins

quick idea

Glittering Heart Card
Create an elegant card by working a heart filled with gleaming gold beads and ivory pearls – see 39 for full instructions.

1 Lay one piece of the silk dupion over the template on page 116 and trace the design using a water-soluble marker. Back the silk with white cotton fabric and stretch in an embroidery hoop (see page 20).

2 Thread a beading needle with a double length of ivory sewing thread and secure with two small backstitches on the reverse side of the fabric. Bring the needle out at the top 'V' on the heart. Pick up one large pearl and one small pearl, and repeat until there are 19 small and 19 large pearls on the thread. Bring the threaded sewing needle out just below the first pearl and couch between each pearl (see couching page 22).

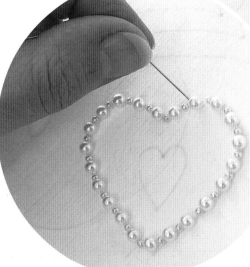

3 Add or remove pearls so that there are enough to complete the heart and then take the beading needle to the reverse side. Finish couching between the last few pearls.

4 Thread a beading needle with a double length of sewing thread and secure on the reverse side near the top of a small heart. Bring the beading needle out at the 'V' of the smaller heart. Pick up one vanilla seed bead and one small pearl, and repeat until there are approximately 13 of each bead. Couch the beads down along the marked line and secure threads on the reverse side.

5 Bring a threaded beading needle out in the centre of the small heart. Pick up a petite crystal bead and take the needle back through, close to where it emerged. Continue adding one petite bead at a time until the area is completely filled. Secure the thread on the reverse side.

Alter the spacing between the pearls very slightly so the heart shape or the diamond pattern of alternating beads is continuous.

6 Complete the other corner heart motifs in the same way and then use the same techniques to complete the design. Outline the remaining small hearts and outer diamond-shaped line with vanilla seed beads and small pearls. Fill the next diamond line with alternate large and small pearls and the two inner lines with vanilla seed beads and small pearls. Fill in the hearts and between the two inner lines with petite crystal beads.

7 Iron the interfacing on to the back of the remaining square of silk dupion. Mark a 23cm (9in) square and cut out. Remove the beaded panel from the embroidery hoop, spray with water to remove the water-soluble marker lines and press around the beaded design carefully. Mark a 20cm (8in) square on the back of the bead panel and add a 1.5cm (⅝in) seam allowance all round. Cut along the seam allowance line.

luxurious lace pillow

8 To make up the pillow, place the beaded fabric and silk right sides together and machine stitch along the marked line on the bead panel, leaving a gap on one side for turning. Trim across the corners and turn through. Fill the pillow with stuffing, insert a pot-pourri or herb sachet and slipstitch the gap.

9 Trim the lace seam allowances to 6mm (¼in). Lay the medium width lace on top of the wide lace. Fold under the seam allowance of the narrow lace and pin on top of the other two. Mark the lace into four sections with pins. Set the sewing machine to a long stitch and stitch along the join of the lace, stopping and restarting threads at each pin.

Marking the lace into quarters makes it easier to gather, giving a more even result on the finished pillow.

10 Gather the lace up so there is about 30cm (12in) between the sections. Pin the lace around the pillow front, so the ends are in the centre of one side and the gathered threads are in the middle of each other side. Adjust the gathers and tie the thread ends together. Sew in thread ends and backstitch along the gathered line to secure the lace to the pillow.

11 Cut four 20cm (8in) lengths of cream satin ribbon, tie each in a bow and sew a bow in each corner. Make five organza bows, sew one in the centre and the others on top of the satin bows. To complete, sew pearls and seed beads along the join of the lace border.

quick idea   **Romantic Pouch** *Use the heart template on page 116 to make a ring purse or scented sachet (bead details page 118). Cut a piece of silk large enough to fit in an embroidery hoop, mark the design in the centre and iron interfacing on the back. Work the beading using the pillow techniques. Cut a second piece of silk and with right sides together, stitch the shaped side seams. Trim seams and turn through. Fold the top edge inside, stitch a casing and thread organza ribbon through.*

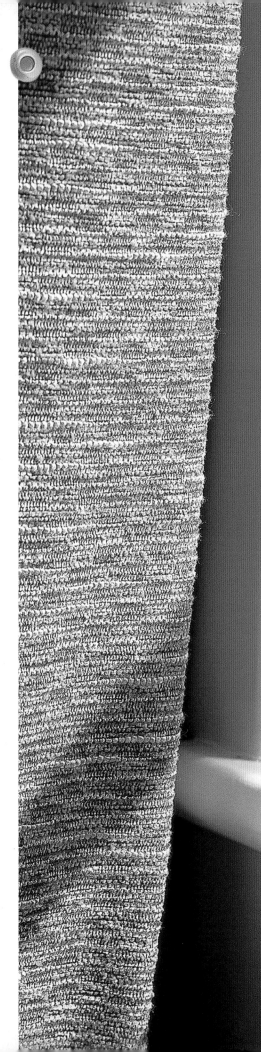

Crazy patchwork frame

A beautiful antique crazy patchwork quilt was the inspiration for this unusual padded picture frame. The subtle blue and lilac silk fabrics have a slightly faded look and tone well, helping to make the different patches work together as a whole design. Whatever fabric colours you use as a background, choose beads that harmonize rather than contrast so that the whole effect is of a slightly aged printed fabric. This frame is quite wide in order that the emphasis is on the bead embroidery but you could alter the proportions to make a larger aperture for a favourite picture or memento.

You will need

(bead details page 118)

- 20cm (8in) square each of blue and light blue silk
- 0.5m (½yd) of lilac silk
- 30cm (12in) square of cotton backing fabric
- two A4 sheets of stiff card
- craft knife and cutting mat
- water-soluble marker
- 5g of size 11 seed beads – frosted denim, ice blue, purple passion, ash mauve and matt lilac
- blue Nymo thread
- matching sewing thread
- size 10 beading needle and a sewing needle
- light blue stranded embroidery cotton (floss)
- 20cm (8in) square of lo-loft wadding (batting)
- wide double-sided adhesive tape
- mount board
- hi-tack glue

1 Trace the template from page 117 on to paper and cut out. Use the paper template to transfer the frame outline on to stiff card and cut out. Mark the position of the diagonal lines on the card.

2 Cut two 20cm (8in) squares from the lilac silk. Using the finished picture as a guide, lay the four squares of silk on the cotton backing fabric so the raw edges overlap. Lay the card frame on top of the silk and mark the position of the diagonal lines with a water-soluble marker. Draw along the edges.

If your fabric is liable to fray easily when cut on the diagonal, iron a lightweight interfacing on the reverse side before you begin.

3 Fold under one edge of each piece of silk along the marked lines, pin and tack (baste). Cut out the centre of the frame leaving at least 1.5cm (⅝in) seam allowance. Tack (baste) along the frame outline and along the aperture lines.

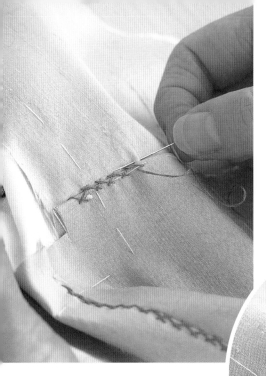

4 Using two strands of light blue embroidery cotton (floss), work a row of herringbone stitch (see right) along all fold lines. Begin and end at least 6mm (¼in) from the tacked (basted) outline. Trace the pattern directly on to the prepared silk panel using a water-soluble marker pen. You can either tape the template and silk on a window or use a light box.

herringbone stitch

5 To begin stitching the bottom left panel, thread a beading needle with Nymo thread and bring the needle up at the end of the first line. Pick up 5 frosted denim seed beads and let them drop down to the fabric. Backstitch through the last two beads. Continue adding 5 beads at a time until you reach the end of the line. Secure the thread on the reverse side.

6 To make the leaves, bring a thread out where the first leaf touches the stem. Pick up 9 ice blue seed beads and take the needle back through at the base of the leaf. Form the loop of beads into a leaf shape and bring the needle out at the top. Pick up one ice blue seed bead and take the needle over the bead loop. Continue working each leaf in the same way.

7 The curved stems of the flowers in the top left area of the frame are worked using couching (see page 22). Thread a beading needle with Nymo thread, secure on the reverse side and bring it out at the end of a curved line. Pick up sufficient purple passion seed beads to fill the line. Bring a threaded sewing needle out at the start of the line and take a tiny stitch over the laid thread between the beads. Continue along the line, couching between every two or three beads.

8 Work the remaining panels of the bead embroidery using the same techniques. Once the panel is complete, spray with water to remove the marker lines. Remove tacking (basting) thread and press around the outside edge.

9 Cut a piece of wadding (batting) the same shape as the card frame and stick in place with double-sided tape. Lay the bead panel face down with the frame on top. Stick double-sided tape around the frame sides. Trim the fabric to 2.5cm (1in) around the edge and the backing about 1cm (½in) smaller. Mitre the corners and stretch on to the frame.

10 Snip into the beaded fabric at the corners of the aperture. Trim the backing fabric to 1cm (½in) and stretch the fabric on to the double-sided tape. Hand sew along the folds of the mitred corners for neatness. Cut a piece of paper with an aperture slightly larger than the card frame and stick on to the back of the stretched fabric to cover the raw edges.

11 To back the frame and make a stand, cut mount board the same size as the frame and a second strip 6 x 18cm (2¼ x 7in). Score across the strip one third of the way down and stick it on the back of the mount board. Spread hi-tack glue along three sides of the mount board, leaving the top edge clear, and then stick it on the back of the frame to finish.

try this *Padded box Make a pretty beaded box using a ready-made box with a lid insert or make a padded box like the one shown here. Cut a piece of silk at least 5cm (2in) larger than the lid, mark the design with a vanishing marker and embroider as in steps 5–8 (bead details page 118). Once beading is complete, trim the fabric to 2.5cm (1in) from the beading and stretch over the lid insert. lacing the edges together in both directions.*

Needle weaving

There is a range of different bead stitches that can be used to make bead fabric and each has a slightly different texture and handle. The three most popular stitches are brick stitch, peyote stitch and square stitch and all three are used in this book. If you have never worked with bead stitches before, you can make some little test panels and use them to create an unusual card or gift tag as shown below. Peyote stitch has been used to make two different styles of scissor keeper (see pages 62 and 67) as well as a beautiful amulet purse (page 72). The beads

Make both panels with the swirls in the same direction – one panel is simply flipped to create the mirror image on the card.

Contrasting swirls

Try your hand at both peyote stitch and brick stitch to make the little bead panels in this pretty card.

You will need

- delicas in red and black
- black Nymo thread
- size 10 beading needle
- 8cm (3¼in) square single-fold white card
- 2.5 x 5.5cm (1 x 2⅛in) rectangles of red and black card
- double-sided tape

Create this card using peyote stitch (page 19) and the amulet purse chart on page 113. The bead strip is only six beads wide, with a row of brick stitch added to balance the pattern. To make a strip, pick up a stop bead and secure (see page 12) and then six red delicas. Pick up another delica, miss one bead and take the needle through the next bead along. Continue picking up one bead and missing a bead to the end of the row. Begin to follow the pattern, adding black beads as shown in the chart. Complete four scroll motifs and finish with two plain rows. Work a row of brick stitch (page 16) down the side of the panel to balance the design. Make a second strip in the opposite colourway and sew in all ends. Stick the black and red card pieces to the front of the white card using double-sided tape, and then tape the two bead panels side by side.

for the purse were chosen to create
a subtle pattern but you can change
the colours for contrast, as shown
in these bold card designs. For best
results, it is always better to use
top quality delica beads for bead
stitches as the beads almost 'snap'
together to create a beautiful fabric.

Use the detailed instructions on
pages 16-19 to try out the different
bead stitches and follow the charts
on page 113 to create the pattern. If
you are familiar with bead stitches
and would like a different challenge,
why not make the crystal necklace
overleaf with its matching earrings?

Musical squares

Make some little square stitch motifs to create this bold card
and tag – an ideal design for a man who loves his music.

You will need

- delicas in gloss black and white
- white Nymo thread
- black paper or card
- music print paper
- 6 x 14cm (2⅜ x 5½in) single-fold red card
- double-sided tape
- 3-d sticky fixers

It is easier to remove the backing paper from double-sided tape if you press the corner down hard on to the beads with a fingernail.

Create this card with little square panels nine beads wide with eight rows. One square has alternate rows of white and black beads, and the other alternates black and white beads to make stripes or checks depending on what bead you start with in each row. If you want to try your own patterns, square stitch designs are easily worked out on graph paper.

Follow the instructions on page 70 to make two different panels of beads for the card. Sew in all thread ends. Cut a 2 x 15cm (¾ x 6in) strip of black paper or card. Cut two 2cm (¾in) squares from one end and use double-sided tape to stick a bead panel to each. Stick the remaining strip on to the red card. Cut two 3.3cm (1¼in) squares of music script paper and stick these over the black strip. Use 3-d sticky fixers to attach the bead panels to the card.

The gift tag is made in the same way from a 5 x 12cm (2 x 4¾in) piece of red card.

Sparkling crystal necklace

Everyone needs at least one impressive necklace for those special occasions that require a little black dress. Not only does this necklace look the part but it is actually quite special too as it contains some unusual square Swarovski crystals. These top quality beads are more commonly found in a round faceted shape but whatever the shape they are renowned for their gorgeous sparkle. The colour range of Swarovski crystals is smaller than seed beads so choose your crystals first and then buy seed beads to match. Finish the necklace with a beautiful fastening and perhaps make a pair of earrings to match (see overleaf).

sparkling crystal necklace

You will need

(bead details page 118)

- Thirty 6mm (¼in) square aquamarine AB Swarovski crystals
- 10g size 10 bright blue AB seed beads
- size 10 beading needle
- monofilament beading thread
- sterling silver necklace crimp fastening
- flat-nosed pliers

quick idea *Sparkly Earrings If you haven't time to make the necklace, you could just work one or two sections of the necklace design and make a pair of earrings instead. Attach two silver jump rings to the top of the bead section and then attach an earring wire.*

1 Cut 1m (1yd) of monofilament and thread the beading needle. Pick up 8 seed beads and take the needle through the first 5 again to form a circle. Push the bead circle down the monofilament leaving a 6cm (15in) tail. Loop the tail through the circle in a single hitch to secure temporarily.

2 Pick up 7 seed beads and feed the needle through the bead where the thread emerged and through the next 4 beads. Repeat this step until there are twenty-five chains (see chain stitch page 17).

3 Pick up a seed bead, a crystal, 3 seed beads, a crystal and a seed bead. Take the needle back through the seed bead where the thread first emerged, then through the next seed bead and the square crystal again. Pull the thread up tight so the crystals are sitting side by side.

4 * Pick up 7 seed beads and feed the needle back through the fourth seed bead from the needle to form a small circle. Pick up 3 seed beads and take the needle back through the crystal.

5 Feed the needle back through the next 3 seed beads and crystal. Repeat from * to create the same pattern on the other side. At this point you need to feed the needle through the seed beads and one of the crystals to emerge out of the centre seed bead opposite the chain. Pick up 7 seed beads and take the needle back through the first 4 beads to form the linking loop.

Nylon monofilament is rather slippery and even secure knots like the double half hitch will tend to pull through. To prevent any problems put a drop of superglue over the knot.

6 Repeat steps 3–5 again fifteen times to create the main body of the necklace. Referring to step 2, work twenty-five loops of chain stitch to complete the necklace. Thread the monofilament tail through the hook part of the necklace fastening. As nylon monofilament is slippery it is better to loop the thread around the hook, back through the last loop of chain stitch and back through the fastening (see also the tip, above). Squeeze the crimp fastening with the tips of flat-nosed pliers and then trim the thread end. Secure the loop part of the fastening to the other end of the necklace to finish.

sparkling crystal necklace

Peacock scissor pendant

Embroidery scissors have a habit of
going walkabout and as they are so small
can prove to be surprisingly elusive.
This elegant little pouch is the ideal
solution as it can be worn like a pendant
necklace and the peyote stitch fabric is
so strong that there is no possibility
of the sharp points protruding through.
The pendant has been cleverly designed
so there is no awkward shaping. The
design is worked in two stages, with the
shaped top sections worked after the main
body is complete. As a result you only
need to shape the pendant with simple
decreasing at the beginning of each row.

You will need
(bead details page 118)

- 10g delicas in metallic matt rose/green
- 5g each delicas – matt black, silver-lined blue zircon, silver-lined aquamarine, galvanized metallic green and galvanized metallic medium green
- black quilting thread
- size 10 beading needle
- embroidery scissors

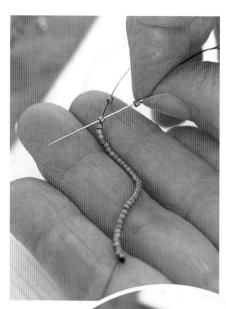

1 Thread a beading needle with a long length of quilting thread. Begin the peyote stitch with a stop bead (see page 12). Pick up a contrast bead, drop it down to the last 15cm (6in) and take the needle through twice. Pick up 36 rose/green delicas. Work peyote stitch, (page 19) picking up another rose/green delica and take the needle through the second delica from the end. Pick up another delica, miss one and take the needle through the next delica along. Repeat this pattern to the end. Pull up the thread and beads tightly.

2 Pick up a rose/green delica and take the needle into the first dropped-down delica. Repeat to the end. On the next row begin to follow the chart on page 116, from the wavy line down, adding 7 rose/green delicas then 4 black delicas in the middle of the row, and then the remaining 7 rose/green delicas.

3 Continue following the chart, taking note that you are adding a bead in between beads from the previous row. To shape the sides for the first time, complete rows until there are three rose/green delicas on the right-hand side. On the next row do not pick up a delica, but feed the needle through the first dropped-down bead. Continue following the chart to the end of the row and repeat the shaping for the next side at the beginning of the next row.

4 Continue working peyote stitch, following the chart and shaping the sides where indicated until you have completed the pattern down to the bottom. Sew in the thread securely at the bottom of the panel.

5 To work the shaping at the top of the bead panel join on a thread at the right-hand side. Work a row of peyote stitch into the centre of the bead panel. To shape the beginning of the next row, do not pick up a delica but take the needle through the first raised bead.

Weave the Nymo thread back and forwards through the beads at the top 'V' of the shaping to strengthen the panel before working the second side.

6 Continue shaping the inside edge until only one bead is left. Repeat the process in reverse to complete the other side of the panel.

Work a second bead panel to match the first. Sew in any side threads, leaving the long tails at the top of the side seams on one of the panels.

7 Lay one bead panel on top of the other, matching the shaping. Pick up one rose/green delica and take the needle through the first two loops of thread at the edge of the panels. Continue picking up one delica at a time to sew the side edges together all the way round.

8 To make the chain strap, pick up 2 rose/green delicas, 2 galvanized metallic green delicas, 2 rose/green delicas and then another 2 galvanized metallic green delicas. Tie the beads into a circle and then take the needle back through the first 6 beads again (see chain stitch page 17).

9 Pick up 2 silver-lined blue zircon delicas, 2 rose/green delicas and 2 more silver-lined blue delicas. Feed the needle back through the top two rose/green delicas from the previous circle and the next four delicas. Continue working chain stitch until the strap is the length required.

10 Sew one end of the chain into one side of the scissor keeper, sewing the thread through the chain and the top of the scissor keeper several times to make a strong join. Secure the end with a double half hitch (see page 23) and feed the thread through several beads on the scissor keeper before snipping off the end. Join the other end of the chain in the same way.

try this *Scissor Keeper This little sewing accessory is made from a panel of peyote stitch (page 19), 3 x 6cm (1¼ x 2½in). Begin with a stop bead (page 12) and pick up 10 black delicas, a rose/green delica and a further 11 black delicas. On the next row only pick up black delicas and work peyote stitch to the end then pull the beads up tightly. Work from the chart on page 116 until the panel is complete. Join the ends together in a tube (see page 19) and then sew one side seam. Make or buy a length of fine black cord. Stuff the pouch with polyester stuffing and hold the two sides together to make a lozenge shape. Tuck the knotted cord in one corner and stitch the seam to finish.*

Retro torque

Whether you are an original hippy chick or like the current retro fashions, this necklace is for you. Although the beautiful tubular beads were inspired by those amazing black and white abstract patterns from the 1960s, the gorgeous necklace is quite contemporary. Known as a torque, these necklaces can be solid silver-plated wire or intertwined sterling silver wire like this one, which is flexible. The beads are worked in square stitch, which looks like bead loom weaving, so designs can be planned on graph paper. The delica beads are tubular and evenly sized and slot together neatly to create the bead fabric. Choose your favourite pattern and make a set of earrings too.

retro torque

You will need

(bead details page 118)

- 2g matt white delicas
- 2g matt black delicas
- five 10mm (⅜in) bone discs
- white Nymo thread
- size 10 beading needle
- sterling silver torque necklace

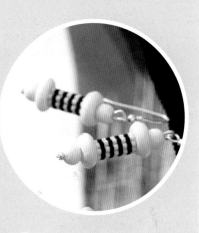

quick idea

Retro Earrings *Make a pair of funky earrings to match the necklace. Simply choose your favourite tubular bead pattern and make two matching tubes, just like the necklace. Cut a 10cm (4in) length of 0.7mm (22swg) silver-plated wire and feed a small ivory bead on to one end. Bend the wire over to secure. Pick up a bone disc and then the bead tube, another ivory disc and a small ivory bead. Bend the wire around the tip of round-nosed pliers to form a ring and snip off the excess wire. Open out the ring on an earring wire, fit the earring in and close the ring again. Make a second earring in the same way.*

1 Thread a beading needle with a 1.5m (1¾yd) length of Nymo thread. Following chart D on page 115 (charts are shown in the order seen in the necklace photograph), pick up 2 white and 2 black delicas and repeat the sequence until there are 10 beads on the thread. Let the beads drop down to leave a 15cm (6in) tail.

2 Hold the tail securely in your hand and pick up a white delica. Take the needle back through the previous white delica and the one just added, so the bead is suspended below the first row (see square stitch page 18).

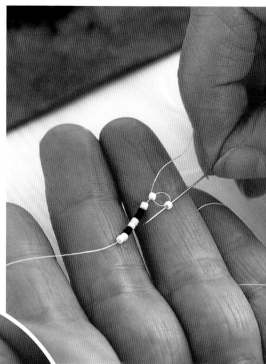

3 Pick up a second white delica and take the needle back through the next bead on the top row then through the bead just added. Continue along the row, adding beads that match the one above in the previous row. At the end of the row, take the needle back along the first row and then along the second row to reinforce the beading.

70 needle weaving

4 On the next row reverse the bead order and begin with 2 black delicas, working rows of square stitch from the chart until you have completed eight rows. Remember to take the needle and thread back through the previous row and the one just worked to reinforce the stitching at the end of each row.

5 To join the seams, fold the bead panel in half and work the same stitch through the two rows of beads without adding any further beads. Tie off the threads using a surgeon's knot (see page 23) and feed the threads back down a row of beads before trimming the ends.

Use a bead rasp to enlarge the bead hole if it is too small to feed the torque through.

6 Following the bead charts A, B and C on page 115, make three more tubular beads. Feed a bone disc on to the torque and then a tubular bead. Repeat until the necklace has 4 tubular beads and 5 bone discs.

If the torque wire is fine you will need to support the shape of the tubes with sections of black plastic straw or rolled black paper. Simply feed the bead tubes over the straw sections and secure with a drop of superglue.

Mardi Gras amulet bag

An amulet is a good luck charm and these little bags were traditionally made to hold one so the wearer was protected from evil spirits. Nowadays the pretty bags are often worn as a pendant necklace and, although very small, are still large enough for some coins, so you are never left stranded. This bag features bright beads in Mardi Gras colours and is worked in peyote stitch with a subtle coil pattern created by following a chart. To complement the bead pattern, the bag has a little coiled wire fastening and is finished with a pretty neck strap interspersed with gorgeous spiral wire beads.

You will need

(bead details page 118)

- 5g each size 11 seed beads – Mardi Gras red, royal plum and cinnamon red
- red quilting thread
- size 10 beading needle
- fine crochet hook or knitting needle
- 3m (3¼yd) of 0.5mm (25swg) pink enamelled wire
- wire cutters
- round-nosed pliers

quick idea

Spiral Wire Necklace
If you don't have time to make the amulet purse, why not just create a simple necklace using the carnival-bright spiral wire beads? Just follow step 5 and then add a necklace fastening.

1 Thread the beading needle with a 1m (1yd) length of quilting thread. Following the chart on page 113, begin peyote stitch (page 19) by picking up an odd bead as a stop bead and letting it drop down to 15cm (6in) from the end. Take the needle through the stop bead twice. Mix the cinnamon red and royal plum beads on a beading mat and then pick up 30 with the threaded needle. Pick up another bead and feed the needle through the second last bead from the end.

When following the bead chart it can help to line a ruler up along the row you are working and then move it down one row at a time.

2 Pick up another seed bead, miss one and take the needle through the next seed bead along. Repeat this pattern to the end. Pull up the thread and beads tightly. On the third row of peyote stitch, using the same bead mix, put the needle through every dropped-down bead. On the fourth row begin to follow the pattern from the top wavy line on the chart, alternating the seed bead mix with Mardi Gras red.

3 Continue working peyote stitch following the chart. When you reach the bottom wavy line, start again at the very top of the chart and work down to the bottom wavy line again. To create the flap of the purse, decrease one bead at the beginning of each row. To do this do not pick up a seed bead but take the needle through the first dropped-down bead. Continue the pattern as shown on the chart, to the end.

4 Sew in any side threads on the bead panel. To balance the panel add a row of brick stitch (see page 16) down the left-hand side. Secure a thread at the top left-hand side and pick up 2 seed beads from the seed bead mix. Take the needle through the first thread loop at the side and back through the second bead added. Pick up a seed bead, go under the next thread loop and back through the bead. Continue working peyote stitch down to the beginning of the shaping. Sew in the thread end.

5 To make the metal decoration for the purse flap, cut a 10cm (4in) length of pink wire. Hold one end in the round-nosed pliers and bend round to form a ring. Hold the ring between finger and thumb and bend the wire round to begin to form a coil. Keep moving the coil round and bending the wire until the coil is 6mm (¼in) in diameter. Feed on a 1.2cm (½in) length of spiral wire and then coil the other end to match. Sew the decoration to the end of the flap.

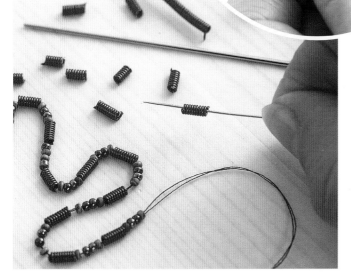

6 To make the neck chain, hold the end of the pink wire against a crochet hook and wind the wire around the handle to form a tight coil. Snip the coil into 6mm (¼in) lengths. You will need about 50 spiral wire beads for the chain. Thread a beading needle with a long length of red thread and pick up a Mardi Gras red bead, 2 mixed seed beads, a Mardi Gras bead and a pink spiral. Repeat until the neck chain is the desired length.

7 Fold the bead panel up to form a square bag shape. To sew the side seams, secure a thread at the top edge and oversew through each pair of threads down the side. For extra strength, work back up to form tiny cross stitches and sew in the end securely. Stitch both side seams and then sew the strap to the top of the side seams. Work the thread back and forth through the beads before snipping off the end.

Fringing, netting

Fringing, netting and tassels are all different beading techniques but are grouped together here because they are all created from beads strung on to thread. Fringes and tassels are similar: tassels have beads strands in a bundle while fringes have strands of beads in a line. The beaded tassels on page 84 are really just fringing in a circle! Netting, on the other hand, is created from a mesh of threads covered in beads and is often finished with fringing or tassels. The beaded baubles on page 90 show just how sensational these three techniques can be. If you think they are a bit

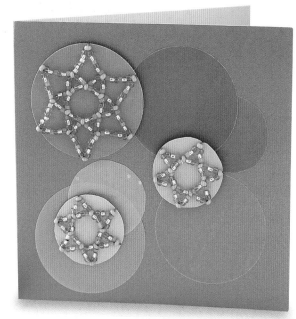

Use a low-tack tape to hold the threads and beads in position while you work on other strands.

Super stars

Create a beaded stars card from coordinating beads, using silver-lined or metallic beads for sparkle – the ideal way to try the net beading technique before making the baubles on page 90.

You will need

- 0.3mm (30swg) silver-plated wire
- 2g each of size 8 purple seed beads in transparent, silver-lined, porcelain, alabaster and hex
- white quilting thread
- size 10 beading needles
- embroidery scissors
- craft scissors
- 12.5cm (5in) square pearlescent blue card
- coloured vellums in blues and purples
- double-sided tape
- 3-d sticky fixers

Create this card by first making the beaded star motifs using the method described in the bauble steps 1–5 on page 92. The small stars have one row of netting added to the initial ring of beads, and the larger star has two rows.

The stars are mounted on circles of card so they hold their shape. The size of the circles will depend on the exact size of beads used for the project. For size 8 beads use 5cm (2in) and 3.2cm (1¼in) diameter circles. Cut circles in different shades of vellum and stick on to a pearlescent card. Attach the beaded circles with 3-d sticky fixers.

and tassels

daunting, try the netting technique by making the star card shown below. Fringing has been used for many years as an embellishment for furnishings, clothes and bags and it's delightful how the beads catch the light as the strands swing from side to side. Try a small sample of fringing on a card for a party-loving teenager before moving on to the gorgeous beaded bags overleaf - choose from a simple single fringe or a stunning evening bag in true Charleston style. Whichever bag you decide to make, remember to use a cord thread so the fringes dangle and swing delectably.

Feathered fringe

This fun and frivolous card is perfect for a teenager who likes fashion and accessories. Tall cards are very popular and only need a short length of fringing.

You will need

- 2g each of size 8 purple seed beads in silver-lined and hex
- white quilting thread
- size 10 beading needles
- embroidery scissors
- 1.2cm (½in) wide double-sided adhesive tape
- piece of marabou feather trim
- 21 x 7.5cm (8¼ x 3in) single-fold card

Spread the marabou feathers out on the reverse side to reveal as much of the core as possible before sticking it down.

Create this card by first sticking two pieces of double-sided tape across the card about 7cm (2¾in) from the top edge. Stick the thread end to the double-sided tape. Pick up 6 hex beads and a silver-lined bead, repeat twice and then pick up 3 silver lined beads. Take the needle back through the strand of hex beads. Stick the thread to the double-sided tape so the beads touch the bottom edge. On the next strand, pick up 3 hex and a silver-lined bead, 6 hex and a silver-lined bead, twice, and then 3 hex. Miss the last hex and take the needle back up the bead strand. Repeat these two strands across the card.

Apply tape to the top of the threads. Cut the marabou feather to the same width as the card and press down to secure.

Marabou charleston bag

This jaunty little bag will have you dancing the night away in the most elegant fashion. It is made from a luxurious heavyweight silk dupion which has been lined with an iron-on interfacing to support the bead fringing. This bag can be made with any size of seed bead but you will need to increase the number of beads on each strand if you choose smaller beads than the size 8 used in this project. If time is short, you don't have to cover the bag in beads but can simply work one row of bead fringing along the top edge and then finish with a marabou feather trim, as shown on page 83.

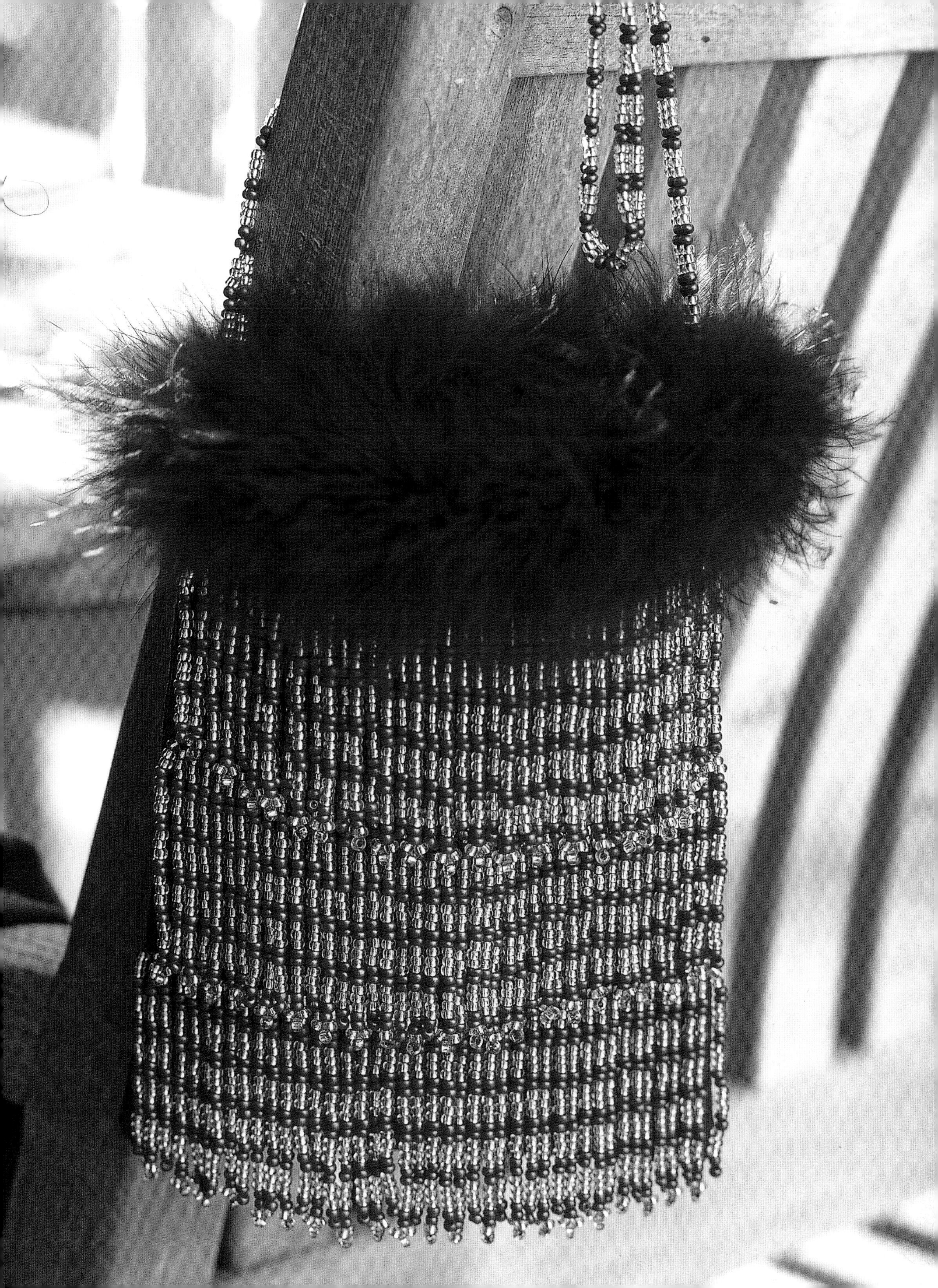

You will need

(bead details page 118)

- 32 x 37cm (12½ x 14½in) wine heavyweight silk dupion
- 32 x 37cm (12½ x 14½in) medium weight iron-on interfacing
- 50g size 8 silver-lined pink seed beads
- 40g size 8 Ceylon wine seed beads
- wine quilting thread
- two size 10 beading needles
- pencil and ruler
- marabou feather trim, about 60cm (24in)

quick idea *Feather Fringe Card Work just a small section of bead fringe to create this fluffy card, described on page 77.*

1 Cut two 16 x 37cm (6¼ x 14½in) pieces of silk dupion. Cut two pieces of interfacing the same size and iron on to the back of the silk. With right sides together, sew around the pieces, leaving a gap on one long side near the corner.

2 Trim across the corners and trim the seams to 6mm (¼in). Turn the bag through and ease out the corners at the opposite end to the gap. Press the bag flat at that end so the seams are exactly on the edge. Slipstitch the gap and tuck the other end inside to create the lining. Press the top edge.

3 Mark the position of the beading at each side of the bag: 1.5cm (⅝in) down from the top edge, then 6cm (2⅜in) down from the first marks and 5cm (2in) down from the second marks. Mark a row of dots 6mm (¼in) apart along the bag, level with the marks.

4 Thread a beading needle with a double length of quilting thread and secure with two tiny backstitches 3mm (⅛in) in from the edge of the bag at the row of dots. Pick up 3 silver-lined beads and 2 wine beads. Repeat five times then pick up 3 more silver-lined beads. Take the needle back up through the last 2 wine beads and the rest of the fringe strand.

When working the beading, select only the fattest beads so that each fringe strand is the same length.

5 Take the needle back in where it emerged and along between the layers of fabric to the first dot. Pick up the same sequence of beads, but instead of picking up the last 3 silver-lined beads, miss the last wine bead and take the needle back up the fringe strand. Repeat these two strands, sewing one *between* the dots and the next *on* the dot, to the end of the row.

To avoid any stitching showing on the inside of the bag when attaching the fringe, carefully stitch through the top layer of fabric only.

6 On the second and the third rows of fringing, work only five repeats in all. Alternate the two strand endings as before until all the fringing is complete. Take care to sew in the ends of the threads securely at the end of each row of fringing.

7 Cut a piece of feather trim to fit around the top of the bag. Begin at the back, oversewing the trim and avoiding thread showing on the inside of the bag. Oversew the end securely and trim any excess.

8 To make the strap, cut two double lengths of quilting thread and thread each pair into a beading needle. Tie the ends together and leave a tail for sewing in. Pick up 3 silver-lined beads and 2 wine beads on each needle. Take one needle back through the wine beads on the opposite strand and then back through the wine beads on the first strand.

9 Repeat the sequence, alternating the thread that goes through the wine beads each time until the strap is the length required. Attach the straps by sewing a pair of thread ends into the bag at the top of each side.

try this *Wedding Bag This handbag version of the Charleston bag would be ideal for a bride or bridesmaid. It is much quicker to make as it has only one row of fringing, although you could easily continue the fringing across the back too. Make the bag in the same way as the main project but work only one row of fringing. Make a handle the length you require from tiger tail wire, feeding sufficient seed beads on to the wire to cover it. Attach the ends of the wire securely to the front of the bag so they will be hidden under the feather trim. Make a handle for the back in the same way and then oversew the marabou feather trim all around the top edge.*

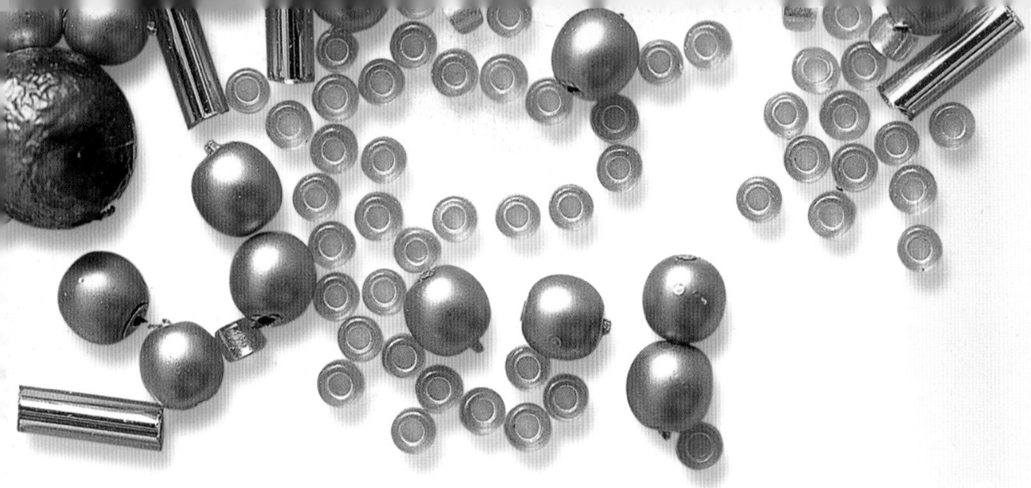

Ornate baroque tassels

Tassels are one of the most decorative and elegant elements of soft furnishing and can be used to add a finishing touch to anything from a cushion to a table runner or as an opulent tieback for curtains, as shown here. These stunning tassels are formed by attaching beads over a wooden tassel top, which forms the shape of the head, with the fringe then worked separately and added around the bottom. Choose various sizes of glass seed beads to cover the tassel top, taking into account its shape and size, and use some of the larger beads on the end of the fringe.

You will need

(bead details page 118)

- two 7.5cm (3in) long wooden tassel tops
- ten (approx) 8mm dark gold ice pearl beads
- nine (approx) 8mm light gold ice pearl beads
- 50g 4mm gold pearls
- 30g size 9 gold seed beads
- 20g 7mm gold bugles
- 20g 10mm gold bugles
- 5m (5yd) of 0.45mm (26swg) gold-plated wire
- 5m (5yd) of 0.2mm (36swg) silver-plated wire
- hi-tack glue
- 2m (2yd) of 4cm (1½in) wide gold organza ribbon
- masking tape
- white quilting thread

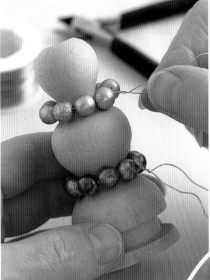

2 Pick up enough 4mm gold pearls on lengths of gold-plated wire to fit around the tassel top above and below the two rows of large beads. Secure the beads as before and repeat the process with gold seed beads, tying these above and below the small gold pearls.

1 Pick up about 10 dark gold ice pearl beads on a 20cm (8in) length of 0.45mm (26swg) gold-plated wire. Wrap the beads around the lower neck of the tassel top and check the fit. Twist the wires together, trim to 6mm (¼in) and tuck the ends in behind the beads. Tie light gold ice pearl beads around the top neck in the same way.

3 Cut a 2m (2¼yd) length of 0.2mm (36swg) silver-plated wire. Start working ladder stitch (see instructions page 17), picking up 2 7mm bugles and letting them drop into the middle of the wire. Feed the wire through the second bead from the opposite direction and pull tight. Thread a wire through each end of another bugle and pull tight. Repeat until there is a strip long enough to fit around the middle of the tassel top. Make a strip of 10mm bugles in the same way, to fit around the base of the tassel top.

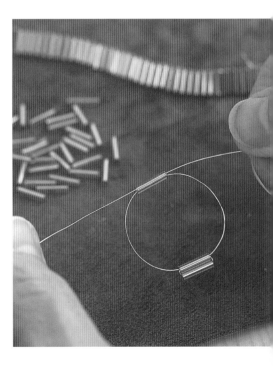

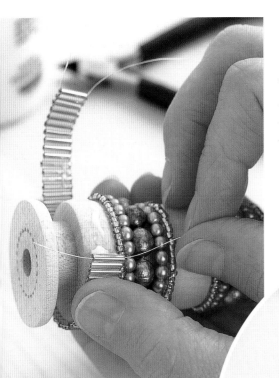

4 Spread a thin layer of hi-tack glue around the base of the tassel top and press the 10mm bugle strip in place. To join the ends, feed the wires back through the first bugle and through the second bugle again. Trim the ends neatly. Glue the 7mm bugle strip around the middle of the tassel top in the same way.

Tassel tops are available in a variety of shapes and sizes, simply attach the first row in one of the 'necks' and work out from there.

5 Add rows of seed beads if necessary to fill any gaps between the bugle strips. Make progressively shorter lengths of seed beads to cover the dome at the top of the tassel and glue these in position as before. Thread the gold organza ribbon through the hole using a wire 'needle'. Tie the end around a large ice bead and tuck the tail of the ribbon back into the tassel head to secure.

6 Cut a 30cm (12in) length of 0.45mm (26swg) gold-plated wire and fold in half. Use masking tape to fix the wire to the work surface. To begin the fringe strands for the tassel, cut a long length of quilting thread and feed the ends into a needle. Take the needle under the wire and through the loop at the end of the thread. This thread will make several fringe strands and then another can be joined on.

7 Pick up 5 gold seed beads, a 7mm bugle, 7 seed beads, a 7mm bugle, 9 seed beads, a 10mm bugle, 11 seed beads, a 4mm gold pearl and a light gold ice bead. Pick up a seed bead and take the needle back through the gold ice bead and the rest of the beads on the fringe strand.

8 Loop the thread around the wire in a half hitch and then pick up the same sequence of beads for the next strand, this time missing out the large ice bead. Continue alternating the two strands and also alternate the ice beads from light to dark along the wire.

9 Work about 40 fringe strands along the length of the wire. Take the fringe wire and wrap it around the lower channel in the tassel top, twisting the wire ends together and trimming neatly. Using the gold-plated wire, fit a row of gold pearls into the channel to finish. Make a second tassel to match the first and attach to the other end of the ribbon. Wrap the ribbon around the curtains and tie in a bow.

try this *Exotic Tassel Rather than beading the fringe you can finish the tassels with thread or raffia for a softer effect. Bead tassels can also be embellished with a feather trim which will contrast with the shiny beads and create a fabulously contemporary look. See page 118 for bead details.*

Glittering baubles

Why should a bauble be seen just at
Christmas? These exquisitely beaded
baubles are so gorgeous you'll be
reluctant to put then away with the rest
of the decorations. Each bauble is made
from the same basic beaded net, which is
worked flat on a work surface and then
finished in slightly different ways to
create two designs (see also another
variation on page 95). Choose five beads
of similar size that match the colour
of your bauble and tone well together.
Remember that the baubles are made of
glass and should be handled with care
once the net and fringing is completed.

You will need

for the purple bauble
(bead details page 118)

- 15cm (6in) of 0.3mm (30swg) silver-plated wire
- 15g each size 8 seed beads – transparent purple, silver-lined purple, porcelain purple, alabaster purple and purple hex beads
- white quilting thread
- size 10 long and short beading needles
- embroidery scissors
- craft scissors

quick idea **Super stars card** *A card decorated with pretty net stars could be given at any time of year – see full instructions on page 76.*

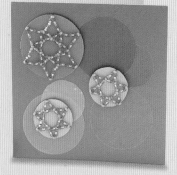

1 Cut a 30cm (12in) length of wire and pick up the following sequence of beads: silver-lined, alabaster, transparent and porcelain – referred to for the rest of the project as [s,a,t,p]. If you have different beads, arrange them in order and label them with these names on the beading mat to make it easier to follow the pattern. Repeat the sequence five times so there are 24 beads on the wire. Feed one end of the wire through all the beads again, pull tight and then twist the ends together and trim.

2 Cut six 1m (39in) lengths of white quilting thread and feed one thread through each alabaster bead, pulling halfway through so all the ends are at the same level. Thread a beading needle on to one of the thread ends and pick up a hex bead, a silver-lined bead, a hex, and then an alabaster seed bead.

Use a short beading needle to work the netting and a long beading needle to work the fringing on the baubles.

3 Thread a needle on the next thread along (not the other end of the previous thread). Pick up a hex, a silver-lined bead and a hex. Take the needle through the last bead from the previous thread to create the first point of a star shape. Move to the next two threads and repeat the process. Continue until all the threads are beaded and there are six points in a star shape.

4 On the second round, pick up 7 beads on the first thread: hex, [s,a,t,p] hex and silver-lined. On the next thread round (from the next point), pick up the first 6 beads in the same order as before. Take the thread back through the last silver-lined bead. Repeat all the way round. On the third round, pick up 11 beads on one thread (hex, [s,a,t,p], [s,a,t,p], hex and alabaster) and thread the first 10 on the next thread. Complete in the same way as the previous round.

5 At this stage you should have a large star shape with six points. This time, working with a pair of threads from one point, pick up 8 alabaster beads on the left-hand thread. Go back through the first 4 beads again with the same thread. Take the other thread through the second 4 beads. Feed both threads through an alabaster bead. On the next point repeat with silver-lined beads and finish with an alabaster bead at the bottom. Alternate these loops all the way round.

6 Working with one thread from adjacent points again, begin to reverse the shaping. Pick up a hex [s,a,t,p], [s,a,t,p], hex and alabaster. On the next thread pick up the first 9 beads and take the needle through the last alabaster in the same direction so the hole is vertical. Repeat all the way round.

7 Working with the pairs of thread from the alabaster beads, pick up 6 beads on each thread: hex, [s,a,t,p] and hex. At this stage it is a good ideal to drape the net over the bauble to check the fit and alter the number of beads just added so they will fit into another beaded wire ring.

8 Make a wire ring as in step 1. Take one thread end through an alabaster bead, secure with a double half hitch (see page 23) and feed the thread around the ring to the next alabaster bead. Take the other thread end from the pair and feed through the next alabaster bead, secure with a half hitch and again feed through to the next alabaster bead. Repeat so there are three adjacent pairs of threads secured.

9 Slip the net over the bauble and secure the remaining three pairs of threads on the ring, so there are pairs of threads coming out either side of the six alabaster beads.

10 To make a fringe strand, use one thread and pick up a hex and [s,a,t,p] six times in all so there are 30 beads on the string. Pick up 4 silver-lined beads and feed the thread back up several beads. Work a half hitch to secure and feed the needle up several more beads, leaving a tail. Bring the next thread down through the bead string and feed through the 4 silver-lined beads again. Pick up 2 silver-lined beads, take the needle between the threads at the bottom of the previous 4 beads and pick up another 2 silver-lined beads. Finish the berry by taking the needle down through 2 beads, picking up 2 silver-lined beads and feeding the needle back through to the strand. Secure as before and trim ends. Make five more strands this way.

11 To fill the large net holes, feed a 50cm (20in) length of quilting thread through the top silver-lined bead in each net. Using both threads together, pick up a hex, [s,a,t,p], silver and alabaster. Make a loop with 8 porcelain beads as step 5 and pull the loop tight. Make a second loop with 8 transparent beads. Pick up [s,a,t,p], silver and alabaster and feed the threads through the alabaster bead at the bottom of the net hole. Secure threads. Repeat in each large net hole.

 try this *Frosted Rose Bauble Once you have made the first bauble it is quite easy to vary the net pattern to create a more ornate net. Just begin with the star as before and then experiment, adding extra threads if required. This pink bauble is finished with fringe strands added higher up the bauble, while the blue bauble (shown on page 91) has a small beaded tassel instead.*

Bead wirework

Teaming wire and beads immediately gives a contemporary look to any project and as wire is now available in a wide range of colours, you can make projects to suit any décor or colour scheme. The type of wire used for the projects in this book is enamelled copper wire which is available in a range of thicknesses and is easy to cut and handle. It is possible to make wire projects without any special tools, but it is worth investing in a set of jewellery tools that are not expensive but which will make your work much neater. The little swirl cards shown below will give you

If you don't have deckle-edged scissors simply tear the vellum carefully to create a similar effect.

You will need

- 0.5mm (25swg) turquoise wire
- eight 4mm turquoise crystals
- ten size 11 blue seed beads
- wire cutters
- round-nose pliers
- superglue gel
- 14.5 x 8cm (5¾ x 3in) single-fold cream pearlescent card
- gold script vellum
- small pieces of blue and copper pearlescent card
- double-sided tape
- 3-d sticky fixers

Bead swirls

A tiny piece of wire and some matching beads are all you need to embellish this quick and easy card.

Create this card by first cutting two 12cm (4¾in) lengths of wire, coiling one end of each using round-nose pliers. Beginning with a seed bead, feed on alternate crystals and seed beads until there are 4 crystals on each wire. Coil up the second end and adjust the swirls if required. Apply a dot of superglue at each end to secure the beads in position. Cut two 4cm (1½in) squares of turquoise card and two 2 x 4cm (¾ x 1½in) rectangles in copper. Stick the copper card on to the squares so one edge juts out. Glue the bead motifs to the panels with dots of glue. Cut a 4cm (1½in) wide piece of gold script vellum using deckle-edged scissors and stick across the card. Attach the swirls using 3-d fixers.

Make a 12 x 5.5cm (4¾ x 2⅛in) gift tag using the same techniques.

practice handling wire so that you can move with confidence on to the nightlight holders shown overleaf. Of course if you are short of time, use your new skills to make some pretty cards instead. The butterfly card shown uses similar techniques to the dragonfly pin on page 108, and both are interchangeable - you could easily have a couple of butterflies on your hat instead. And talking of headwear, tiaras have become an essential wedding accessory. The design on page 102 is ideal for a winter wedding or would look stunning for a 'posh' evening event.

Beaded butterfly

Use two tones of enamelled wire to create a pretty beaded butterfly which can be used to decorate a card or gift box.

You will need

- 0.7mm (22swg) blue enamelled wire
- 0.5mm (25swg) blue and supa grey enamelled wire
- wire cutters
- round-nose pliers
- size nine blue seed beads
- ten 4mm (5/32in) turquoise crystals
- size 10 knitting needle
- 10.5 x 15cm (4⅛ x 5¾in) single-fold turquoise pearlescent card
- label motif print paper
- double-sided tape
- craft glue dots

Create this card featuring a butterfly made in a similar way to the dragonfly on page 108. To make the wings, cut 50cm (20in) of 0.7mm wire, pick up 50 seed beads, let them drop down to 10cm (4in) from one end and twist together to form a loop. Pick up 50 beads and twist again to make the second wing. Repeat to make the two lower wings. Twist the ends together and bend up to make feelers, trim the ends to the same length and coil them. Shape the wings by hand. Join on a length of 0.5mm blue wire and wrap it around the first wing from side to side. Weave the wire down the middle adding 2 crystals as you go. Repeat for each wing. Make a body and head as in steps 4 and 5 on page 111. Wire the body to the wings.

To make the card, tear down one edge of some label print paper and stick to the card front, to about halfway across. Trim all paper edges and stick the butterfly on with craft glue dots.

Pour a small amount of seed beads into your cupped hand to make it quicker and easier to pick beads up on the wire.

Shimmering tea light

A table lit with candles creates a wonderfully romantic atmosphere but tall candlesticks, although elegant, can be easily knocked over. These stunning tea lights are the perfect, safe alternative as each candle is enclosed in a coloured-glass votive (candle holder) which can be decorated with beads, crystals and wire to suit your décor. Whatever colour scheme you choose, you should have no problem finding three toning wires in a light, medium and dark shade to suit the glass colour as there are many colours of enamelled wire available. The wire embellishments also make striking earrings - see page 100.

You will need

(bead details page 118)

- Glass votive (candle holder)
- 2.5m (2¾yd) of 0.7mm (22 swg) enamelled copper wire in aqua
- 1.5m (1½yd) of 0.7mm (22 swg) enamelled copper wire in blue/green and blue
- 1m (1yd) of 0.315mm (30 swg) silver-plated wire
- wire cutters
- flat-nosed and round-nosed pliers
- round wire jig and pegs (see page 7 and step 5)
- gel superglue
- 1g each size 11 seed beads in crystal, blue iris and rainbow
- 75 (approx) 4mm crystals each clear, blue and aqua

quick idea *Spiral Earrings If short of time, or you want to give a guest a surprise gift, make a pair of fun drop earrings. Just follow steps 3–6 of the tea lights, then attach silver earring wires.*

1 Cut 1m (1yd) of pale grey/green wire and fold in half. Secure the cut ends in a vice or get a friend to hold with flat-nosed pliers and twist using a spinster (see page 7). Form the wire into a circle to fit round the votive and wrap the ends once. Snip one piece of wire from each end, wrap the single wire around the circle several times and trim off the excess.

If you don't have a spinster you can twist the wire using a hand drill with a cup hook fitted in the chub.

2 On a 1m (1yd) length of silver-plated wire pick up a rainbow seed bead, a blue/green and a crystal seed bead; repeat about fifteen times. Attach the fine wire to the wire ring and begin to wrap the fine wire around the ring, trapping a seed bead about every 5mm (³⁄₁₆in). Add more beads until the ring is covered and then snip off excess wire.

To keep the beads from slipping down the bent or coiled wire, apply a drop of superglue or other high-tack glue under the first seed bead.

3 To make the spiralled wires, cut three or four 12cm (5in) lengths of 0.7mm wire in each colour. Make a small circle at one end of the wire with the round-nosed pliers. Hold the circle in the flat-nosed pliers and bend the wire round to form a coil. Keep moving the pliers round and bending the wire to leave a 6cm (2½in) tail. Repeat for all wires.

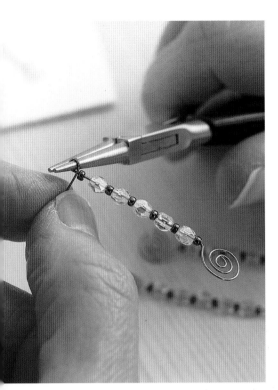

4 Bend the tail of a blue wire at 45 degrees and apply a dot of glue just above the bend. Pick up a rainbow seed bead and a blue crystal and repeat until there are 5 crystals and 6 seed beads. Leave the glue to dry. Use round-nosed pliers to make a ring at the end of the wire and then trim off excess wire. Make three or four beaded wires in this way in each wire colour: with silver wire use crystal seed beads and clear crystals; with aqua wire use blue/green seed beads and green crystals.

5 To make the curved S-shaped wires, set the pegs into the round wire jig as shown. Wrap a length of blue wire around the top peg and loop around each peg working down to the bottom and straight out around the last peg. Lift the formed wire off and trim the tail to 5cm (2in). Make three or four in each wire colour, depending on the size of your candle holder.

6 Apply a dot of glue on the bottom bend of the blue wire. Pick up 5 rainbow seed beads, a blue crystal and a rainbow seed bead. Put to one side until the glue has set. Use round-nosed pliers to make a small ring on the end and trim excess wire. Decorate the other wire colours in the same way, using the colour combinations given at the end of step 4.

Always take care never to leave lighted candles unattended.

7 Hook one of the coiled and beaded wire pieces between two beads on the wire ring and squeeze the ends together with the flat-nosed pliers. Miss two beads and attach one of the bent wire pieces in the same way. Work around the ring alternating the styles and mixing the colours. Fit the ring over the votive to finish.

shimmering tea light 101

Wild berry tiara

Tiaras have become quite fashionable in recent years and although usually worn by brides or bridesmaids, they can be quite fun to wear at elegant parties. This tiara has an unusual autumnal look with its beautiful beaded berries and bugle leaves and was inspired by the way brambles twist and tangle in the hedgerows. It would be ideal for a winter party or an autumn wedding but would look just as stunning made in more traditional colours of white and cream. If you find the idea of a tiara a little daunting, make a small spray like the one shown on page 107. This can be attached to a bag or hat or worn as a corsage on a wedding outfit.

You will need
(bead details page 119)

- 1m (1yd) of 0.9mm (20swg) dark purple enamelled wire
- 2m (2yd) of 0.2mm (36swg) dark purple enamelled wire
- 3m (3yd) of 0.7mm (22swg) leaf green enamelled wire
- 3m (3yd) of 0.315mm (30swg) leaf green enamelled wire
- 5g each size 11 seed beads – wild blueberry, heather mauve and matt lilac
- 5g each size 11 seed beads – brilliant shamrock, citron and autumn green
- 3g each 6mm and 9mm bugle beads in willow
- 3g each 9mm and 14mm bugle beads in rainbow
- four 1.2cm (½in) diameter purple beads for berry centres
- flat-nosed and round-nosed pliers
- wire cutters

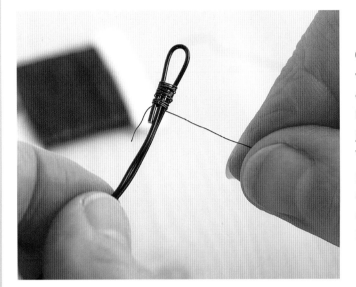

1 Cut two 40cm (16in) lengths of 0.9mm dark purple wire. Bend 1cm (½in) over at one end and lay the second length just into the loop. Wrap 0.2mm dark purple wire tightly around to cover the cut ends, leaving a loop for hairpins.

2 Wrap the fine wire in a more open manner to hold the two thicker wires together. At the other end, bend one wire over again and trim the second length if required. Wrap the cut ends tightly and then tie off the fine wire and trim neatly. Bend the wire into a hairband shape to create the tiara base.

3 To make a leaf, cut a 25cm (10in) length of 0.7mm leaf green wire. Using flat-nosed pliers, bend over 8cm (3in) from one end to make the top point of the leaf shape. Bend the wire again about 1cm (½in) either side of the point. Bend the wire about 6mm (¼in) away to make the next two points. Make the lower points slightly longer again. Finally, bend the wire at 90 degrees to finish creating the leaf shape.

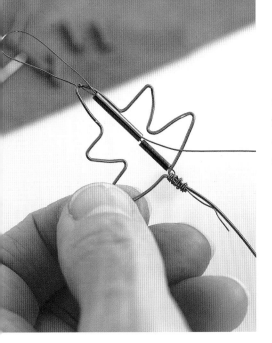

4 Trim the short end of the leaf shape to 6mm (¼in). Wrap the finer 0.315mm leaf green wire, around the leaf shape base to secure. Pick up a 9mm willow bugle and a 14mm rainbow bugle on the long end of the fine wire. Wrap the wire around the top point of the leaf twice and then feed it back through the longer bugle. Pick up a 9mm willow bugle and wrap the wire around one of the middle points on the leaf. Feed the wire back down the bugle. Continue adding bugle beads to create the veins of the leaf and then snip off any excess fine wire.

5 To make a berry, tie the end of a 1m (1yd) length of 0.2mm purple wire through the hole of one of the large purple beads. Pick up 8 heather mauve seed beads and feed the wire back through the hole. Continue adding 8 beads at time until there are eight or nine rows. Finish covering the bead with a row of wild blueberry beads between every two rows of heather mauve.

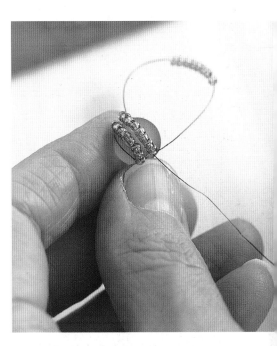

6 Create lifelike texture on the berry by picking up individual beads on the wire and looping the wire under the previous bead strands. Work all over the berry using all three purple bead colours randomly. At some point, add two or three beads at a time to cover the hole at the top.

7 Cut a 25cm (10in) length of 0.7mm leaf green wire. Bend one end over to make a 6mm (¼in) loop and feed it inside the berry. Wrap the end of the fine wire around the wire stem to secure.

8 Hold the bramble against the leaf stem and twist the wires together for about 2cm (¾in). Make the long tail into a slightly smaller leaf shape and then use short bugles to make the veins on this leaf, as in step 4. Make two more large berry stems with two leaves each. Make two smaller stems with only one small leaf on each.

9 To make small leaf sprays, cut a length of 0.315mm leaf green wire. Pick up 8 green seed beads in a random order. Bend the wires over to form a loop of beads and twist the wires together to create the top leaf. Pick up 8 more beads to make a second loop and then 8 more to make a third loop on the other side. Twist the ends of the wires together a few times and then make the last two leaves with 10 seed beads.

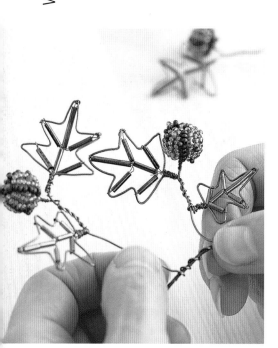

10 To make wire tendrils, cut 15cm (6in) of 0.9mm purple wire. Hold each end of the wire with round-nosed pliers and bend around to make a small loop. Wrap the wire around a rod or knitting needle to create a loose spiral at each end. Make four double tendrils in all.

11 To assemble the tiara, take one of the larger stems and holding it in the middle of the tiara base, wind the tail around to secure. Secure one of the other large stems on one side.

Build the tiara up gradually, adding berries, leaves and wire tendrils until you achieve a balanced effect.

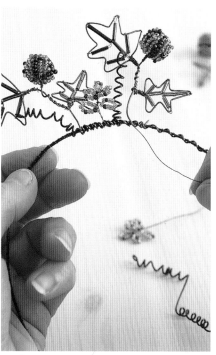

12 Wind one or two tendrils around between the berry stems with spiral ends facing upwards. Add a small leaf spray in between. Add another large berry spray on the other side and then shape the tiara with two smaller sprays at the end. Fill in with tendrils and leaf sprays to complete.

try this **Bridal Spray** *Make a single berry spray with gold-coloured wire and cream, gold and white beads and sew it securely to the front of a small silk bag. See bead details page 119.*

Dragonfly pin

Don't you love lazy summer days when you can have a picnic by the local river or pond and watch the dragonflies flitting back and forth across the water? These exquisite dragonflies look very realistic although they are made entirely in wire and beads, with their delicate wings formed from a fine metallic ribbon. You can make your dragonflies in realistic colours as shown overleaf or make them to match your favourite outfit. Glue a brooch pin to the back of the dragonfly so it can be worn as a brooch, or simply push a hatpin through the wires at the back and pin it to a pretty summer hat.

You will need
(bead details page 119)

- 11 seed beads size 11 – antique cranberry, desert peach, cherry sorbet and ice
- 16 petite seed beads in ice
- two 6mm (¼in) burgundy crystals
- 2m (2yd) of 0.45mm (26swg) enamelled copper wire in wine, pink and silver
- 50cm (20in) of 0.8mm (21swg) silver-plated wire
- 50cm (20in) of 0.2mm (36swg) silver-plated wire
- 25cm (10in) of 9mm (⅜in) wide silver metallic ribbon
- size 11 knitting needle
- flat-nosed pliers and wire cutters
- micro glue dots
- hatpin

quick idea *Dragonfly Brooch Use some gorgeous iridescent bead colours to make this realistic dragonfly which can be attached to a little purse, bag or jacket (see bead details page 119).*

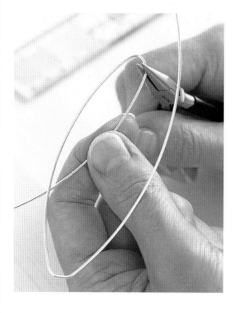

1 Cut a 50cm (20in) length of 0.8mm silver-plated wire. To create the wing shape, hold the wire in the middle and bend it over the pliers about 4.5cm (1¾in) from the centre point in each direction. Use the pliers to make a slight bend on the bottom edge near the tip, to give wings an authentic look.

2 Bend the wires up at 90 degrees in the middle and fold over the top of the wings. Bend out again at 90 degrees below the wings ready to make the second set of wings. Shape the lower wings so they are slightly longer and deeper than the top wings. When you bring the wires into the centre again, twist the ends together, bend up and wind one end over the top wings to secure. Snip off excess wire.

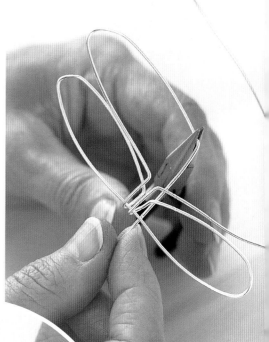

Use a desk magnifying lamp to see the tiny loops of wire more clearly when you are gathering the tubes of wire mesh.

3 Cut four 5–6cm (2–2½in) lengths of silver metallic ribbon. Unravel one end of each length slightly, thread the tail end into a needle and feed through the loops. Pull up to gather the end and then sew in to secure. Slide the ribbon lengths over the wings so they all meet in the middle. Sew together with fine wire.

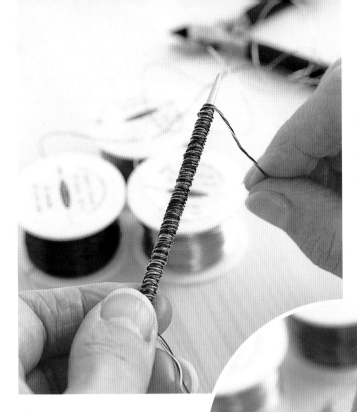

4 Hold all three colours of the 0.45mm enamelled wires together and wind around the knitting needle. Begin about 8cm (3in) from the end and keep wrapping right to the end of the point. Snip the wires neatly at both ends.

5 Feed 0.45mm pink and silver wires through the two burgundy crystals and pull the wires together so the crystals lie side by side. Wrap the long end of the wires around the tail and then over the top between the beads several times to create the head of the dragonfly. Feed the tail end into the top of the wrapped wire body and wrap the long end around several times to secure. Snip off the ends neatly.

6 On the wine wire, pick up 16 petite ice beads, 11 ice, 11 desert peach, 11 cherry sorbet and 11 antique cranberry seed beads. Beginning with cherry sorbet, repeat the beads in the reverse order. Secure the end of the wire just below the head. Wrap the beaded wire around the body to create the abdomen.

7 Lay the body on the wings and wrap the silver-plated wire around and between the wings to secure to the body. As a finishing touch, apply a tiny amount of glue, such as micro dots, on individual petite beads and stick to the wings. Finally, feed a hatpin through the back of the dragonfly or attach a brooch fastening with epoxy resin glue.

charts and diagrams

The chart keys have the bead code numbers, as listed in Bead Project Details on pages 118 and 119. Diagrams are given actual size.

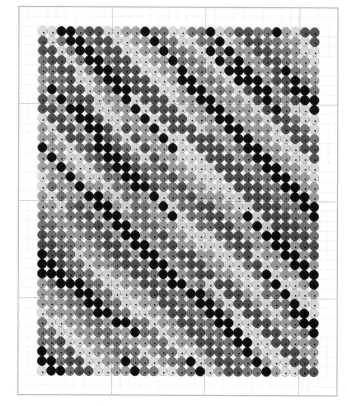

Vibrant Cushion (page 26)
blue colourway chart

- 239
- 057
- 787
- 756
- 076

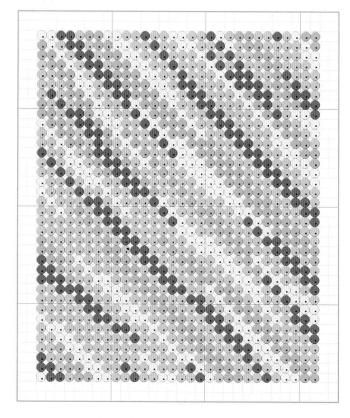

Vibrant Cushion (page 29)
pink colourway chart

- 245
- 236
- 444
- 151
- 682

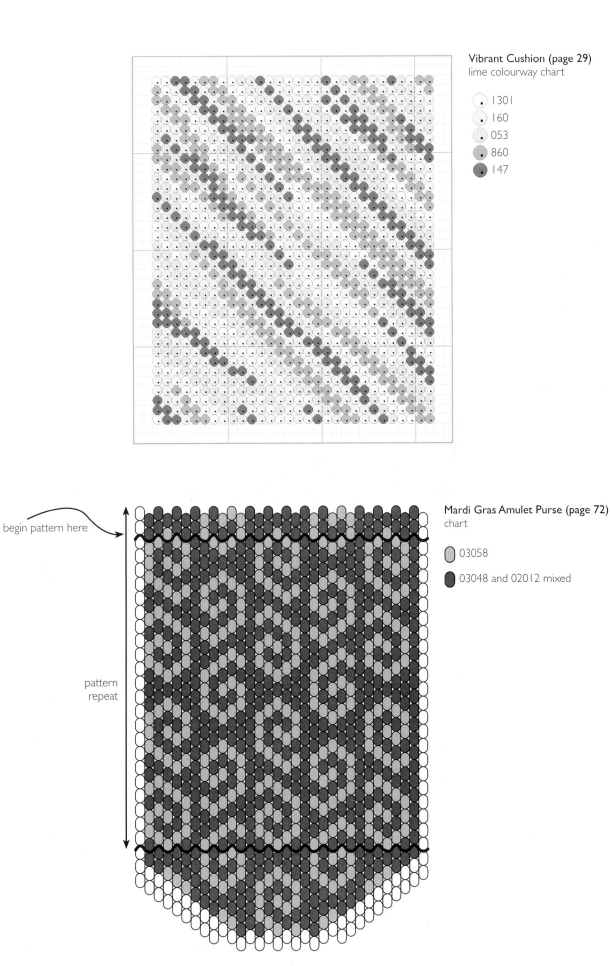

Vibrant Cushion (page 29)
lime colourway chart

- · 1301
- · 160
- · 053
- · 860
- · 147

begin pattern here →

pattern repeat

Mardi Gras Amulet Purse (page 72)
chart

- ◯ 03058
- ● 03048 and 02012 mixed

Antique Velvet Pouch (page 30)
chart

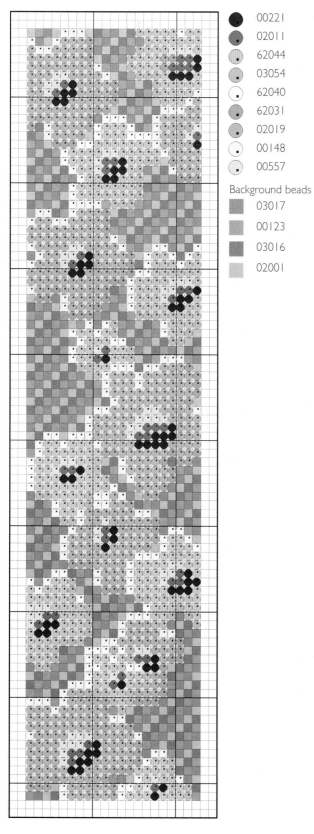

- ● 00221
- ◉ 02011
- ◉ 62044
- ◉ 03054
- ○ 62040
- ○ 62031
- ○ 02019
- ○ 00148
- ○ 00557

Background beads
- ▦ 03017
- ▦ 00123
- ▦ 03016
- ▦ 02001

Mackintosh Rose Album (page 34)
chart

- ● 010
- ● 247
- ◉ 056
- ◉ 003

Luxurious Lace Pillow (page 44)
full size diagram

Retro Torque (page 68)
charts

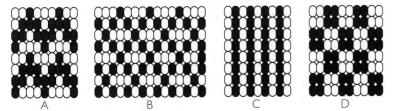

A B C D

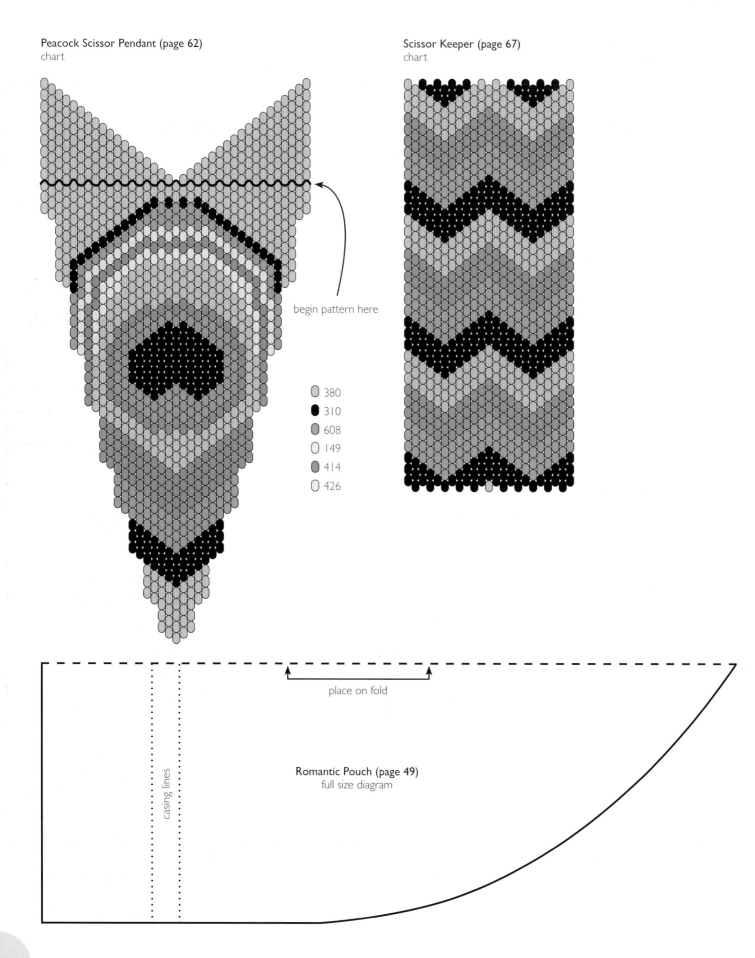

Peacock Scissor Pendant (page 62)
chart

Scissor Keeper (page 67)
chart

begin pattern here

○ 380
● 310
◐ 608
○ 149
◐ 414
○ 426

place on fold

casing lines

Romantic Pouch (page 49)
full size diagram

bead project details

This list contains details of the various beads used in the projects, giving their colours and codes. Unless stated otherwise, the additional ideas and variations provided throughout the book use the same beads as their main projects. The availability of beads can change, however, so the suppliers on page 119 should help you source a vast variety of beads and accessories.

Vibrant Cushion (page 26)
The Spellbound Bead Company –
Miyuki delica beads in lined sky blue
AB 057, lined light blue AB 076,
lined crystal light aquamarine 239
and dyed matt transparent
aquamarine 787.
Jules Gems – delica beads in matt
opaque royal blue 756.
Pink cushion (page 29)
Delica beads in lined crystal medium
pink 245, lined crystal rose lustre 236,
transparent tangerine AB 151, semi-
matt silver-lined orange 682 and matt
transparent orange 744.
Lime cushion (page 29)
Delica beads in dyed transparent light
yellow 1301, lined pale yellow 053,
silver-lined chartreuse 147, opaque
yellow AB 160 and matt chartreuse
AB 860.

Antique Velvet Pouch (page 30)
Mill Hill – size 11 seed beads in pale
peach 00148, crystal honey 02019,
frosted gold 62031, frosted apricot
62040, frosted autumn 62044, desert
sand 03054, gold 00557, Victorian gold
02011, bronze 00221, pearl 02001,
cream 00123, peachy blush 03017 and
vanilla 03016.

Mackintosh Rose Album (page 34)
The Bead Shop, Nottingham – delicas in
black 010, lined magenta AB 056, lined
crystal fuchsia 247 and green iris 003.

Sumptuous Gift Bags (page 40)
The Bead Shop, Nottingham – size 10
pink-lined seed beads;
pink-lined 7mm bugles;
4mm square beads in pink-lined and
bright blue.
Constellation Beads – size 10 bright blue
seed beads;
bright blue 7mm bugles.

Luxurious Lace Pillow (page 44)
Creative Beadcraft – 3mm ivory pearls
and 1.5mm cream pearls
Mill Hill – size 11 seed beads vanilla
03016;
petite crystal 40161.
Romantic Pouch (page 49)
3mm pink pearls, 1.5mm pink pearls,
1.5mm cream pearls and petite seed
beads pink 42018.

Crazy Patchwork Frame (page 50)
Mill Hill – size 11 seed beads in frosted
denim 62043, ice blue 02006, purple
passion 03053, ash mauve 00151 and
matt lilac 02081.
Padded Box (page 55)
Mill Hill size 11 seed beads in heather
mauve 02024 and frosted tea rose
62004.

Sparkling Crystal Necklace (page 58)
The Bead Shop, Nottingham – 6mm
(¼in) square aquamarine AB Swarovski
crystals;
size 10 bright blue AB seed beads.

Peacock Scissor Pendant (page 62)
Beadbox – delicas in metallic matt
rose/green 380.
The Spellbound Bead Company –
delicas in matt black 310, silver-lined
blue zircon 608, silver-lined aquamarine
149, galvanized metallic green 414 and
galvanized metallic medium green 426.

Retro Torque (page 68)
Beadworks – delicas in matt white AD
24, matt black AD 94;
10mm (⅜in) bone discs J20

Mardi Gras Amulet Purse (page 72)
Mill Hill – size 11 seed beads in Mardi
Gras red 03058, royal plum 02012 and
cinnamon red 03048.

Marabou Charleston Bag (page 78)
Rayher – size 8 seed beads in silver-lined
pink and Ceylon wine.

Ornate Baroque Tassels (page 84)
Gütermann – 8mm pearls in dark gold
ice 8940, 8mm pearls in light gold ice
9980 and 4mm pearls in gold 2885;
size 9 seed beads in gold 1870;
7mm and 10mm bugles in gold 1870.
Exotic Tassel (page 89)
Gütermann – size 9 seed beads in pink
4965 and lilac 5865.

Glittering Baubles (page 90)
Rayher – size 8 seed beads in transparent
purple, silver-lined purple, porcelain
purple, alabaster purple and purple hex.
Variations in pink and blue bead ranges
from Rayher.

Shimmering Tea Light (page 98)
Mill Hill – size 11 seed beads in 00161
crystal, 03047 blue iris and 00374
rainbow.
Gütermann – 4mm crystals in clear
1016, blue 6660 and aqua 7080.

Wild Berry Tiara (page 102)
Mill Hill – size 11 seed beads in wild
blueberry 03026, heather mauve 02024,
matt lilac 02081, brilliant shamrock
02054, citron 02031 and autumn green
03029;
bugle beads in willow 72045 and 82045,
and rainbow 82045 and 92045.
Bridal Spray (page 107)
Mill Hill – size 11 seed beads in white
00479, antique champagne 03039 and
cream 00123;
bugle beads in cream 70123, 80123 and
90123.

Dragonfly Pin (page 108)
Mill Hill – size 11 seed beads in antique
cranberry 03003, desert peach 03052,
cherry sorbet 03057 and ice 02010;
petite seed beads in ice 402010.
Gütermann – 6mm (¼in) burgundy
crystals.
Dragonfly Brooch (page 110)
Mill Hill – size 11 seed beads in rainbow
00374, sea breeze 02008, ice green
00561 and ice 02010;
petite seed beads in ice 402010.
Gütermann – 6mm (¼in) burgundy
crystals.

UK

The Bead Shop
104–106 Upper Parliament Street,
Nottingham NG1 6LF
tel: 0115 9588899
email: info@mailorder-beads.co.uk
www.mailorder-beads.co.uk

Beadworks
21a Tower Street, Covent Garden,
London WC2H 9NS
tel: 0207 240 0931
www.beadworks.co.uk

Constellation Beads
PO Box 88, Richmond,
North Yorkshire DL10 4FT
tel: 01748 826552   fax: 01748 826552
email: info@constellationbeads.co.uk
www.constellationbeads.co.uk

Creative Beadcraft
20 Beak Street, London W1R 3HA
tel: 0207 6299964
tel (mail order): 01494 778818
email: beads@creativebeadcraft.co.uk
www.creativebeadcraft.co.uk

Gütermann Beads
Perivale-Gütermann Ltd, Bullsbrook Road,
Hayes, Middlesex UB4 OJR
For nearest stockist tel: 0208 589 1600
UK email: perivale@guetermann.com
Europe email: mail@guetermann.com

Jules Gems
69b Wyle Cop, Bowdler's Passage,
Shrewsbury, Shropshire SY1 1UX
tel: 0845 123 5828   fax: 0845 1235829
email: shop@julesgems.com
www.julesgems.com

Mill Hill Beads
Framecraft Miniatures, Unit 3, Isis House,
Lindon Road, Brownhills, West Midland
WS8 7BW
tel/fax: 01543 360842
tel (international): +44 1543 453154
www.framecraft.com

Ribbon Designs
PO Box 382, Edgware, Middlesex
HA8 7XQ
tel/fax: 0208 958 4966
email: info@silkribbon.co.uk
(Metallic and organza ribbons)

The Scientific Wire Company
18 Raven Road, London E18 1HW
tel: 0208 505 0002   fax: 0208 5591114
www.wires.co.uk

The Spellbound Bead Company
45 Tamworth Street, Lichfield,
Staffordshire WS13 6JW
tel: 01543 417650
www.spellboundbead.co.uk

The Stamp Man
8a Craven Court, High St, Skipton,
North Yorkshire BD23 1DG
tel: 01756 797048
www.thestampman.co.uk
(For photo album kits)

James Hare Silks
PO Box 72, Monarch House,
Queen Street, Leeds LS1 1LX
tel: 0113 243 1204   fax: 0113 243 3525
www.jamessharesilks.co.uk

V V Rouleaux
tel: 0207 7303125
www.vvrouleaux.com
(For ribbons and braids)

Rayher Hobby
Fockestrasse 15, 88471 Laupeim, Germany
tel: 07392 7005 0 fax: 07392 7005 145
email: info@rayher-hobby.de
www.rayher-hobby.de

USA

Beadbox
1290 N. Scotsdale Road, Tempe
AZ 85281-1703
tel: (480) 967-4080
fax: (480) 967-8555
www.beadbox.com

Beadworks
149 Water Street, Norwalk, CT 06854
tel: (203) 852-9108   fax: (203) 855-8015
www.beadworks.com

Gütermann of America Inc
8227 Arrowbridge Boulevard,
PO Box 7387, Charlotte NC 28241-7387
tel: (704) 525-7068
email: info@gutermann-us.com

Mill Hill Beads
For nearest stockist: Gay Bowles Sales Inc
PO Box 1060, Janesville, WI, 53546
tel: (608) 754-9212   fax: (608) 754-0665
www.millhill.com

about the author

Dorothy Wood is a talented and prolific craft maker and author. Since completing a course in Advanced Embroidery and Textiles at Goldsmith's College, London, she has written 17 craft books, and contributed to a further 20, on many subjects. This is Dorothy's fourth book with David & Charles, her first being the best-selling *Simple Glass Beading*. She also contributes to well-known craft magazines including *Crafts Beautiful* and *Card Making and Papercraft*. She lives in Leicestershire, UK.

acknowledgments

Many thanks to the following companies for so generously supplying beads and accessories for this book – Framecraft Miniatures (UK) Ltd, Gay Bowles Inc., Perivale Gütermann, Rayher Hobby and Ribbon Designs. Thanks to the editorial team, Cheryl and Jennifer, who did a superb job of putting the book together, with special thanks to Lin, who has worked so hard to get everything shipshape. Thanks to Simon for the super photography and to designer Prudence, who has made this such a lovely book. Finally I have members of my family to thank – my daughter Barley, who assisted on several of the projects, and my sister Linda, who allowed us to take over her home in Surrey for a few days for the photography.